Brain Box
WOW!
Cool Kid
deep thinking
out of this world
Great idea!
Maths +
excellent!
hidden treasure
WOW!
teacher's pet
so true...
FAB!
Super Star
Know it all!
!
high flyer
time for tea !
!
Maths Whizz
No. 1
Hidden Treasure
out of this world
hard cheese
?
deep thinking
Know it all!
Star pupil
HELP!
Fab at Fractions
GREAT AT GRAPHS
Huh
easy peasy
Great idea!
TOP MARKS
10 out of 10
rocket science
lost the plot
FAB!
time for tea !
?
Fab at Fractions
easy peasy
No. 1
WELL HARD
10 out of 10
TOP MARKS
time for maths
out of this world
puzzled?
out of this world
lost the plot
deep thinking
Maths Whizz
GREAT AT GRAPHS
HELP!
rocket science
over the moon
high flyer
?
FAB!
Maths Whizz
TOP MARKS
time for maths
Hidden Treasure
No. 1
Mega at Maths +
out of this world
Maths Whizz
easy peasy
time for tea!
?
hard cheese
100% maths
TOP MARKS
!
FAB!
WELL HARD
Huh
high flyer
now we're moving
well done!
over the moon
10 out of 10
MEGA
Mega at Maths +
out of this world

Mega Maths

Age 7–9

About this book

Mega Maths offers practice in numeracy skills as described in the guidelines for the National Numeracy Strategy. The book reflects the content of the National Curriculum in England and Wales and the 5–14 Mathematics programme in Scotland.

The book is divided into five sections. Many skills overlap these divisions. We recommend that your child works through the book in the given order. Repetition and practice will help build skills and confidence.

Answers appear on pages 122–128, so that either you or your child can check and mark the work.

How to help your child

Let your child decide how long he or she wants to work on the book. Give lots of encouragement and praise for effort.

Instructions are written clearly and simply, but you may need to look through the activities and explain what your child is being asked to do. If your child has problems with a type of activity, talk about it together and try to help. You may need to discuss it with your child's class teacher.

About the stickers

Your child can add the 100 fun stickers to the pages of the book, or use them to decorate pencil cases, posters or other items.

About the authors

The authors are teachers and educational consultants with many years' experience in schools.

EGMONT
We bring stories to life

First published in Great Britain in 2002 by Egmont UK Limited,
239 Kensington High Street, London W8 6SA
Published in this edition in 2009
© 2009 Egmont UK Limited. All rights reserved
Written by Stephen Rutter, Michael Tonge and Rosemary Wise.
Cover illustration by Craig Cameron, interior illustrations by John Haslam, James Robins and Robin Smythe.
ISBN 978 1 4052 4489 3
3 5 7 9 10 8 6 4
Printed in Italy

Contents

MENTAL MATHS

SHAPES, SPACE and MEASURE

FRACTIONS and DECIMALS

Contents

SOLVING PROBLEMS

CHARTS and GRAPHS

When you add a small number to a large number, put the large number first. It makes counting on easier!

So $135 + 6 = 141$

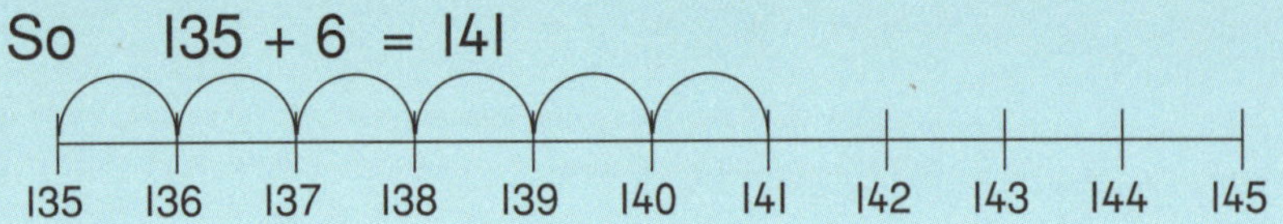

Use the number lines to help you work out these:

Top tip:
When you are counting on, count the jumps, not the numbers themselves.

$78 + 5 = $ _____

77 78 79 80 81 82 83 84 85

$124 + 8 = $ _____

124 125 126 127 128 129 130 131 132

$235 + 7 = $ _____

235 236 237 238 239 240 241 242 243

$337 + 4 = $ _____

337 338 339 340 341 342 343 344 345

You can count on in 10s as well as in 1s:

so $60 + 30 = 90$

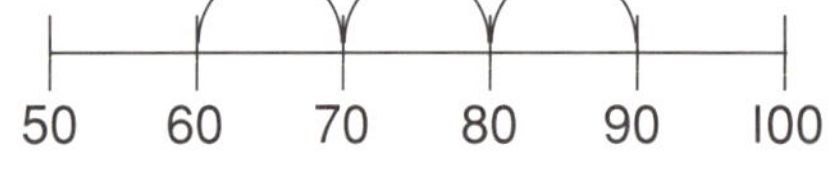

and $76 + 50 = 126$

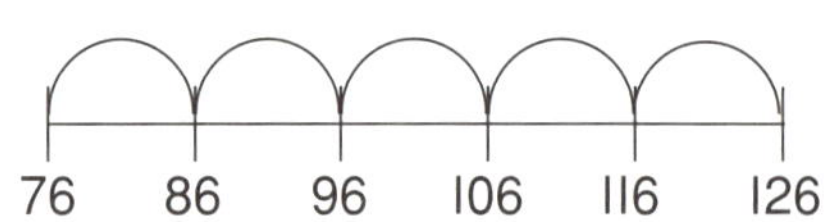

Top tip:
Pick any number you like and count on in 10s – see how far you can get.

Try these:

$85 + 30 = $ _____

65 75 85 95 105 115 125

$124 + 40 = $ _____

124 134 144 154 164 174 184

$68 + 50 = $ _____

68 78 88 98 108 118 128

$95 + 20 = $ _____

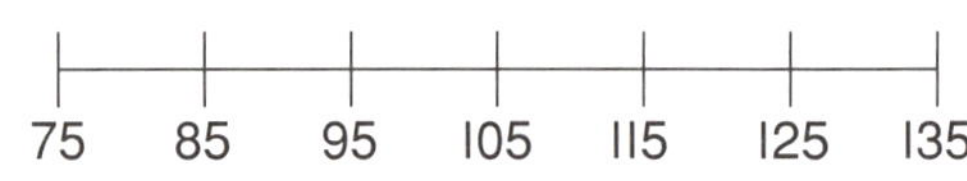

Carry on this pattern:

0,   5,   10,   15,   __,   __,   __,   __,   __,   __

Try counting on in 5s starting from a different number:

8,   13,   18,   23,   28,   33,   __,   __,   __,   __

Can you see a pattern?

Try these:

6,   11,   16,   21,   __,   __,   __,   __,   __,   __

9,   14,   19,   24,   __,   __,   __,   __,   __,   __

7,   12,   17,   22,   __,   __,   __,   __,   __,   __

When you add several numbers together, look for the pairs that make 10:

$$4 + 5 + 3 + 6 + 5$$
$$= (4 + 6) + (5 + 5) + 3$$
$$= 10 + 10 + 3$$
$$= 20 + 3 = 23$$

Top tip:

When you add numbers together you can do it in any order.

Use this method to add these numbers:

3 + 5 + 7 + 5 + 2 = ______________
____
____

6 + 3 + 4 + 1 + 7 = ______________
____
____

Looking for patterns

Top tip:

You can add on 10, 20, 30 and so on to any number. Use this knowledge to add numbers like 9, 19 and 29.

First add the multiple of 10 and then subtract 1, like this: $253 + 9 = 253 + 10 - 1 = 263 - 1 = 262$

$342 + 19 = 342 + 20 - 1 = 362 - 1 = 361$

Try to do these sums in your head. You do not need to write down all the steps.

$56 + 9 = $ _______ $74 + 19 = $ _______

$87 + 29 = $ _______ $63 + 39 = $ _______

$134 + 9 = $ _______ $236 + 19 = $ _______

$323 + 29 = $ _______ $354 + 39 = $ _______

You can use a similar method to add 11, 21, 31 and so on.

$76 + 21 = 76 + 20 + 1 = 96 + 1 = 97$

$365 + 31 = 365 + 30 + 1 = 395 + 1 = 396$

Try these:

$85 + 11 = $ _______ $64 + 21 = $ _______ $58 + 31 = $ _______ $72 + 41 = $ _______

$134 + 11 = $ _______ $435 + 21 = $ _______ $546 + 31 = $ _______ $227 + 41 = $ _______

You can adapt this method if you need to subtract.

$87 - 9 = 87 - 10 + 1 = 77 + 1 = 78$

$126 - 11 = 126 - 10 - 1 = 116 - 1 = 115$

Try these:

$76 - 9 = $ _______ $86 - 19 = $ _______ $154 - 29 = $ _______ $345 - 39 = $ _______

$86 - 11 = $ _______ $93 - 21 = $ _______ $386 - 31 = $ _______ $556 - 41 = $ _______

Looking for patterns

Look at the sums below. See if you can spot the pattern and carry it on:

17 + 5 = 22   87 − 4 = 83

17 + 15 = 32   87 − 14 = 73

17 + 25 = 42   87 − 24 = 63

17 + 35 = _____   87 − 34 = _____

17 + 45 = _____   87 − 44 = _____

17 + 55 = _____   87 − 54 = _____

17 + 65 = _____   87 − 64 = _____

17 + 75 = _____   87 − 74 = _____

17 + 85 = _____   87 − 84 = _____

Top tip:

Always look for patterns in a series of sums. Patterns will help you to solve other sums of the same type.

Look for the pattern in these sums and carry it on:

    5 +   3 =   8
   50 +   30 =   80
  500 +   300 = _____________
 5000 +   3000 = _____________
    7 −   2 =   5
   70 −   20 =   50
  700 −   200 = _____________
 7000 −   2000 = _____________

See if you can spot the pattern in this addition table and complete it:

+	1	2	3	4	5	6	7	8	9	10
1	2	3	4	5	6	7				
2	3	4	5	6	7					
3	4	5	6	7						
4	5	6	7							
5	6	7								
6	7									16
7									16	17
8									17	18
9								17	18	19
10								18	19	20

There are 5 pirate ships.
There are 7 pirates in each ship.
There are 35 pirates altogether, because 7 x 5 = 35.
35 pirates divided between 5 ships gives 7 pirates
on each ship: $35 \div 5 = 7$.

Top tip:

To find the answer to $45 \div 5$, look
in the x5 table until you see the
number 45 and you will see that:
$9 \times 5 = 45$ so $45 \div 5 = 9$

This shows that multiplication and division are the
opposite of each other.

Use the x2, x5 and x10 tables to answer
these division sums:

$20 \div 2 =$ ____________ $16 \div 2 =$ ____________

$40 \div 5 =$ ____________ $25 \div 5 =$ ____________

$40 \div 10 =$ ____________ $60 \div 10 =$ ____________

Divide 18 by 2 ________   Divide 14 by 2 ________

Divide 35 by 5 ________   Divide 15 by 5 ________

Divide 50 by 10 ________   Divide 80 by 10 ________

Halving means dividing by 2. When we want to find half of something we divide it by 2.

What is half of 12? ____________

What is half of 8? ____________

What is half of 20? ____________

Doubling means multiplying by 2.

What is double 6? ____________

What is double 4? ____________

What is double 10? ____________

Show your workings here:

Top tip:

Doubling and halving are the opposite of each other. You can use your multiplication facts to work out sums with bigger numbers.

Carry on counting in 2s to complete this table:

11 x 2 = 22

12 x 2 = 24

13 x 2 = 26

14 x 2 = ____________

15 x 2 = ____________

16 x 2 = ____________

17 x 2 = ____________

18 x 2 = ____________

19 x 2 = ____________

20 x 2 = ____________

Can you spot a pattern here and carry it on?

Half of 22 is 11

Half of 24 is 12

Half of 26 is 13

Half of 28 is ____________

Half of 30 is ____________

Half of 32 is ____________

Half of 34 is ____________

Half of 36 is ____________

Half of 38 is ____________

Half of 40 is ____________

How many of these sums can you answer in
5 minutes?

14 + 16 = ___________   18 + 22 = ___________

35 + 25 = ___________   37 + 23 = ___________

49 + 21 = ___________   48 + 22 = ___________

38 + 32 = ___________   57 + 33 = ___________

63 + 27 = ___________   24 + 66 = ___________

Did you notice anything about all the answers?

Now try again with these. How many can you
get right in 5 minutes? You have to fill in the
missing numbers:

95 + ______ = 100   23 + ______ = 100

60 + ______ = 100   98 + ______ = 100

20 + ______ = 100   88 + ______ = 100

59 + ______ = 100   51 + ______ = 100

40 + ______ = 100   48 + ______ = 100

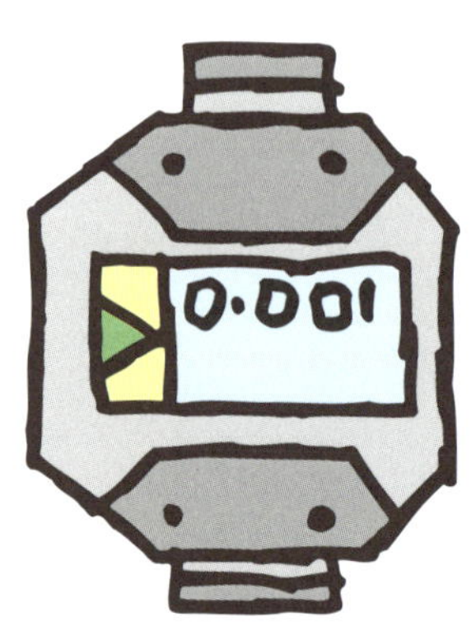

Top tip:

It is important to be able to work
quickly when you want to. The more
you practise the quicker you will get.
But no matter how quick you are,
it only counts if the answers
are right.

Beat the clock

See how many of these
you can do in 5 minutes:

8 x 2 = _______   45 ÷ 5 = _______

6 x 5 = _______   18 ÷ 2 = _______

9 x 10 = _______   50 ÷ 10 = _______

5 x 3 = _______   25 ÷ 5 = _______

2 x 7 = _______   60 ÷ 10 = _______

Show your workings here:

Now try these.
How quickly can you answer them?

23 x 10 = _______   350 ÷ 10 = _______

25 x 2 = _______   34 ÷ 2 = _______

30 x 10 = _______   100 ÷ 2 = _______

14 x 2 = _______   650 ÷ 10 = _______

3 x 100 = _______   700 ÷ 100 = _______

Number facts to 20

You must be able to add together any two numbers
up to 20 + 20, and subtract from any number up to 20.
These are the number facts up to 20.

Decode this secret message by finding the answers and then filling in the letters.

5 + 7	20 − 15	18 − 17	9 + 9	6 + 8	20 − 11	7 + 7	20 − 13
___	___	___	___	___	___	___	___

11 + 9	12 − 4	15 − 10	11 + 8	14 − 9
___	___	___	___	___

14 − 8	18 − 17	12 − 9	3 + 17	12 + 7
___	___	___	___	___

14 − 6	17 − 12	17 − 5	13 + 3	14 + 5
___	___	___	___	___

11 + 9	18 − 3
___	___

6 + 13	9 + 6	20 − 8	11 + 11	19 − 14
___	___	___	___	___

15 − 7	13 − 12	9 + 9	16 − 12	19 − 14	10 + 8
___	___	___	___	___	___

5 + 11	20 − 2	20 − 5	11 − 9	5 + 7	13 − 8	20 − 7	6 + 13
___	___	___	___	___	___	___	___

A	B	C	D	E	F	G	H	I	J	K	L	M
1	2	3	4	5	6	7	8	9	10	11	12	13

N	O	P	Q	R	S	T	U	V	W	X	Y	Z
14	15	16	17	18	19	20	21	22	23	24	25	26

Use your knowledge of number pairs to add up and subtract multiples of 10 and 100.

If 5 + 7 = 12   then 50 + 70 = 120   and 500 + 700 = 1200
if 8 − 3 = 5   then 80 − 30 = 50   and 800 − 300 = 500

Write down the answers to these:

40 + 30 = _____   50 + 90 = _____   60 + 70 = _____   70 + 80 = _____

500 + 600 = _____   600 + 900 = _____   800 + 400 = _____   400 + 300 = _____

60 − 10 = _____   90 − 30 = _____   80 − 40 = _____   100 − 30 = _____

600 − 400 = _____   1200 − 300 = _____   700 − 100 = _____   1500 − 800 = _____

The numbers on the explorers are the answers to the sums on the boats.
Draw lines to join each explorer to the correct boat:

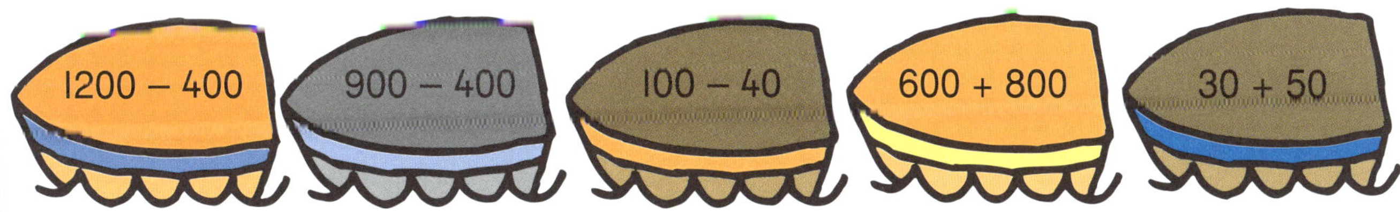

 # Number pairs

You need to be able to recognise the pairs of numbers that make 100.

First try some number pairs that make 10.
Draw a ring round the pairs that make 10:

3 + 7   4 + 8   6 + 5   6 + 4   5 + 5   7 + 4   2 + 8

Now draw rings round the pairs that make 100.

40 + 60   50 + 70   20 + 80

30 + 80   50 + 60   30 + 70

90 + 10   70 + 50   80 + 30

Now you can try some harder ones.
Draw rings round the 100 pairs:

38 + 62   45 + 65   18 + 82

53 + 47   24 + 76   67 + 45

65 + 45   74 + 28   74 + 25

Top tip:
Look at the units first – do they make 10? Then look to see if the tens add up to the remaining 90.
64 + 36 = 100 because 4 + 6 = 10
60 + 30 = 90 and 10 + 90 = 100

I wrote out lots of number pairs on bits of paper but someone tore them up.
Can you draw lines to show which bit of paper goes with which to make 100?

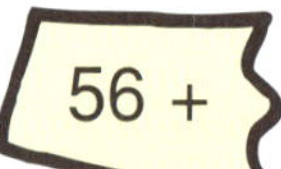

Number pairs

If you know the number pairs that make 100, it is easy to find the pairs that make 1000.

If 60 + 40 = 100   then   600 + 400 = 1000

If 45 + 55 = 100   then   450 + 550 = 1000

Next to each number, write down the number that would make it up to 1000:

500 _____   700 _____   200 _____

950 _____   750 _____   650 _____

Colour in the multiples of 5 to find the hidden number.

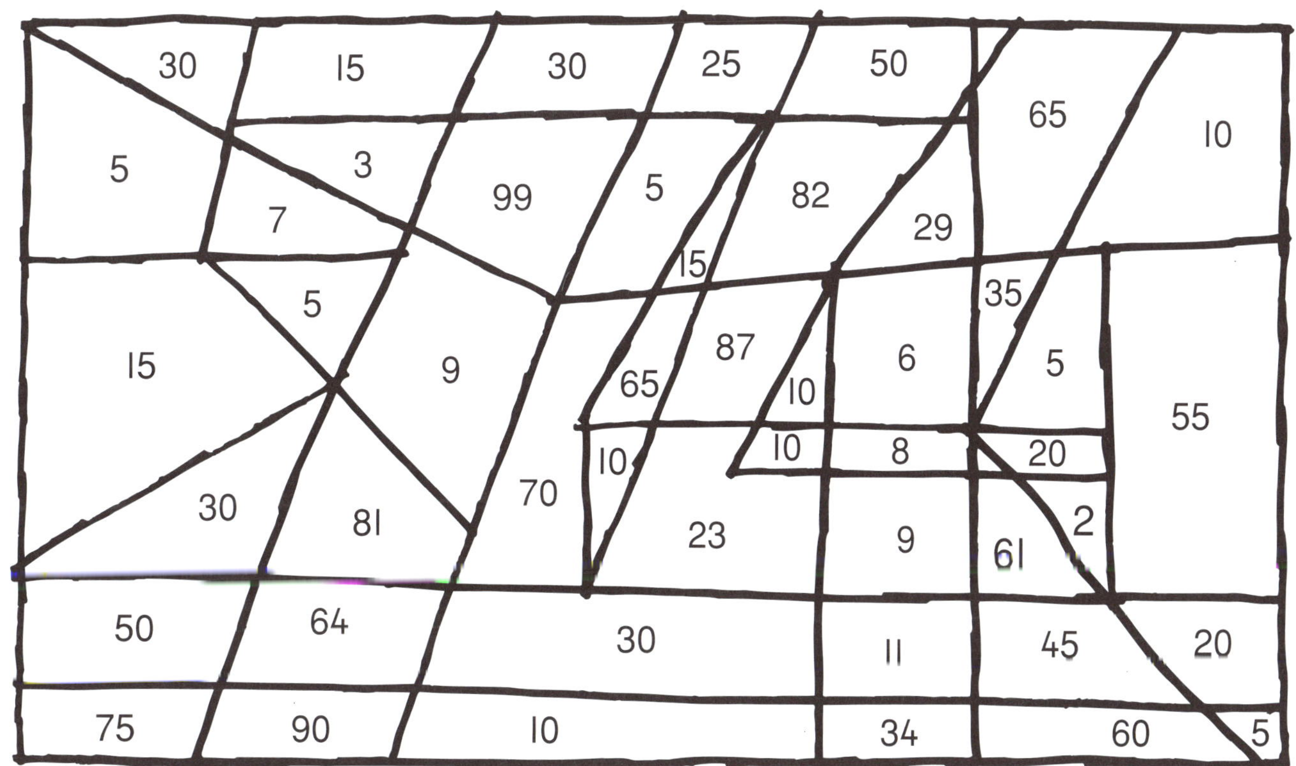

When you have to add a lot of numbers together, remember you can do it in any order.
It helps if you can find pairs of numbers.

$2 + 5 + 9 + 5 + 3 + 1 + 8$ is easier if you do

$2 + 8 = 10$ ➜ $5 + 5 = 10$ ➜ $9 + 1 = 10$ ➜

$10 + 10 + 10 = 30$ ➜ $30 + 3 = 33$

Look for pairs that make 20 or 100:

$17 + 8 + 12 + 3 = (17 + 3) + (8 + 12) = 20 + 20 = 40$

You will not always find easy pairs. Then it is usually best to start with the large numbers and then add the smaller ones:

So $5 + 17 + 7 + 20$ is easier if you do it in the order:

$$20 + 17 = 37$$
$$37 + 7 = 44$$
$$44 + 5 = 49$$

Show your workings here:

Time yourself and see how quickly you can add these up:

$2 + 5 + 8 + 5 = $ ______ $17 + 5 + 3 + 25 = $ ______

$60 + 20 + 40 + 80 = $ ______ $18 + 70 + 2 + 30 = $ ______

$9 + 24 + 5 + 13 = $ ______ $5 + 32 + 23 + 7 = $ ______

$13 + 5 + 7 + 60 + 4 + 6 + 5 = $ ______

To share 3I sweets between 5 people, you can give 6 sweets to each person (5 x 6 = 30), but there is I sweet left over.
We say that there is a remainder of I.

$3I \div 5 = 6$ remainder I $5 \times 6 = 30$ $3I - 30 = I$

or, for short, we write:

$3I \div 5 = 6$ r I

Try these:

$23 \div 2 =$ _____ r _____ $I5 \div 2 =$ _____ r _____ $I3 \div 2 =$ _____ r _____

$27 \div 2 =$ _____ r _____ $34 \div 5 =$ _____ r _____ $43 \div 5 =$ _____ r _____

I2 children want to play five-a-side football.
How many teams will there be? How many children will be left out?

__________ teams   __________ children left over

32 eggs are packed in boxes of 6.
How many full boxes would there be?
How many eggs would be left over?

__________ boxes   __________ eggs left over

45 bottles are packed in crates of I0.
How many crates would there be?
How many bottles would be left over?

__________ crates   __________ bottles left over

I have £5 to share between 4 people:

£5 ÷ 4 = £1 remainder £1

but we can turn the remaining pound into 100p and share that out:

100p ÷ 4 = 25p

so each person ends up with £1 and 25p = £1.25

£5 ÷ 4 = £1.25

Try these:

£7 ÷ 2 = £ _____   £9 ÷ 2 = £ _____   £5 ÷ 2 = £ _____

£9 ÷ 4 = £ _____   £14 ÷ 4 = £ _____   £17 ÷ 4 = £ _____

£16 ÷ 5 = £ _____   £32 ÷ 5 = £ _____   £39 ÷ 4 = £ _____

£32 ÷ 10 = £ _____ £43 ÷ 10 = £ _____ £64 ÷ 10 = £ _____

5 children want to buy a football between them which costs £16.

How much will each child have to pay? _____________________

4 people buy a winning ticket for the lottery.
They win £10 between them.
How much will each person get? _____________________

Mary saves up for 10 weeks to buy a pair of shoes.
The shoes cost £25.
How much must she save each week? _____________________

Do you know your x3 and x4 tables?

Add on in 4s to complete this x4 table:

    0 x 4 = 0

    1 x 4 = 4

    2 x 4 = 8

    3 x 4 = 12

    4 x 4 = _______________

    5 x 4 = _______________

    6 x 4 = _______________

    7 x 4 = _______________

    8 x 4 = _______________

    9 x 4 = _______________

    10 x 4 = _______________

Add on in 3s to complete this x3 table:

    0 x 3 = 0

    1 x 3 = 3

    2 x 3 = 6

    3 x 3 = 9

    4 x 3 = _______________

    5 x 3 = _______________

    6 x 3 = _______________

    7 x 3 = _______________

    8 x 3 = _______________

    9 x 3 = _______________

    10 x 3 = _______________

Top tip:

You need to practise saying your tables until you know them by heart. Remember that multiplication can be done either way round. So when you learn that 6 x 3 = 18 you also know that 3 x 6 = 18!

A group of four explorers have found an ancient tomb.
To open the door they must press the right buttons.

Help the explorers open the door by marking the right buttons with a tick.

To find the right buttons, answer these sums:

7 x 2 =______

6 x 3 =______

8 x 4 =______

10 x 5 =______

9 x 10 =______

When the explorers get through the door, they see an old chest.

To open the chest they must find the right key.

The key to open the chest is in the x3 and x5 tables but not in the x2, x4 or x10 tables.

Which key do they pick?

Times table practice

In the chest the explorers find an old piece of paper. On it is a message in code. Can you solve the puzzle and decode the message?

7 x 4   3 x 3   1 x 5

______ ______ ______

4 x 7   5 x 5   1 x 5   0 x 3   9 x 3   10 x 3   5 x 5   5 x 1

______ ______ ______ ______ ______ ______ ______ ______

5 x 2   3 x 9

______ ______

3 x 3   2 x 5   4 x 1   2 x 2   1 x 5   6 x 3

______ ______ ______ ______ ______ ______

2 x 3   4 x 5   6 x 5   5 x 5

______ ______ ______ ______

7 x 4   5 x 2   4 x 4   5 x 1   3 x 9

______ ______ ______ ______ ______

9 x 3   10 x 1   8 x 5

______ ______ ______

7 x 3   4 x 0   3 x 1   1 x 5   3 x 9

______ ______ ______ ______ ______

6 x 3   5 x 4   5 x 5   4 x 7   3 x 3

______ ______ ______ ______ ______

2 x 10   6 x 1

______ ______

7 x 4   1 x 9   5 x 1

______ ______ ______

5 x 4   5 x 3   2 x 2

______ ______ ______

9 x 3   4 x 7   0 x 5   14 x 2   6 x 5   1 x 5

______ ______ ______ ______ ______ ______

A	B	C	D	E	F	G	H	I	J	K	L	M
0	2	3	4	5	6	8	9	10	12	14	15	16

N	O	P	Q	R	S	T	U	V	W	X	Y	Z
18	20	21	24	25	27	28	30	32	35	40	45	50

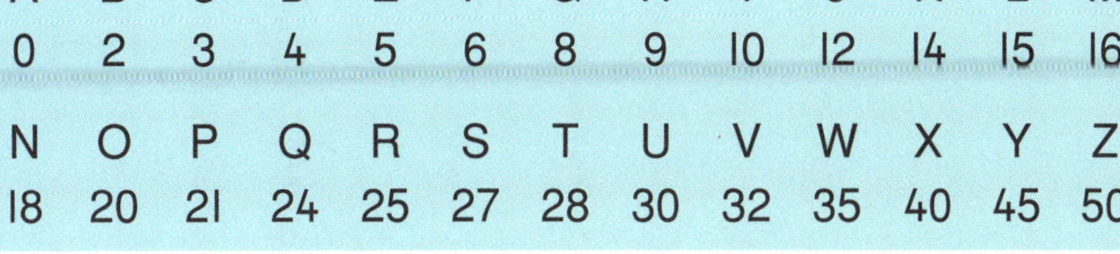

Top tip:

You can use your knowledge of the x2, x3, x4, x5 and x10 tables to do other multiplications.

Show your workings here:

To multiply 2 by 6, multiply by 3 and then by 2.

2 x 6   x 3   6   x 2   12

To multiply by 11, multiply by 10 and then add the number on.

Complete this pattern:

3 x 6   x 3 ___9___   x 2 ___18___

4 x 6   x 3 ______   x 2 ______

5 x 6   x 3 ______   x 2 ______

6 x 6   x 3 ______   x 2 ______

7 x 6   x 3 ______   x 2 ______

8 x 6   x 3 ______   x 2 ______

9 x 6   x 3 ______   x 2 ______

10 x 6   x 3 ______   x 2 ______

Complete this pattern:

3 x 11   30 + 3 =   33

4 x 11   40 + 4 =   44

12 x 11   120 + 12 =   132

6 x 11   _______________

9 x 11   _______________

11 x 11   _______________

14 x 11   _______________

15 x 11   _______________

20 x 11   _______________

19 x 11   _______________

Using facts and adjusting

If you want to multiply by 9 there are two ways you can do it.

1. Multiply by 3 and then by 3 again.

| 8 x 9 | 8 x 3 = 24 | 24 x 3 = 72 |
| 12 x 9 | 12 x 3 = 36 | 36 x 3 = 108 |

2. Multiply by 10 and then subtract the number.

| 8 x 9 | 8 x 10 = 80 | 80 − 8 = 72 |
| 12 x 9 | 12 x 10 = 120 | 120 − 12 = 108 |

Use the first method to calculate:

6 x 9 = __________

7 x 9 = __________

9 x 9 = __________

11 x 9 = __________

15 x 9 = __________

20 x 9 = __________

25 x 9 = __________

Now try the second method:

6 x 9 = __________

7 x 9 = __________

9 x 9 = __________

11 x 9 = __________

15 x 9 = __________

20 x 9 = __________

25 x 9 = __________

Did you get the same answers both times?

Which method do you like best?

Complete the patterns below:

10 x 10 = 100	30 x 10 = 300
11 x 10 = 110	35 x 10 = 350
12 x 10 = 120	40 x 10 =_____________
13 x 10 =_____________	45 x 10 =_____________
14 x 10 =_____________	50 x 10 =_____________
15 x 10 =_____________	55 x 10 =_____________
16 x 10 =_____________	60 x 10 =_____________
17 x 10 =_____________	65 x 10 =_____________
18 x 10 =_____________	70 x 10 =_____________
19 x 10 =_____________	75 x 10 =_____________
20 x 10 =_____________	80 x 10 =_____________

Mercury bars are packed in boxes of 10.
How many bars are there in:

32 boxes? ______   24 boxes?______   48 boxes?______

53 boxes? ______   135 boxes?______   246 boxes?______

The delivery lorries can carry 100 boxes each.
How many boxes are there in:

8 lorries? ______   15 lorries?______   23 lorries?______

54 lorries? ______   68 lorries?______   125 lorries?______

Show your workings here:

How many boxes would you need for:

| 50 bars? | ÷ 10 | = | 5 boxes |

| 120 bars? | ÷ 10 | = | 12 boxes |

380 bars?　______________

470 bars?　______________

1560 bars?　______________

2600 bars?　______________

How many lorries would you need to carry:

| 300 boxes? | ÷ 100 | = | 3 lorries |

| 4500 boxes? | ÷ 100 | = | 45 lorries |

3800 boxes?　______________

2900 boxes?　______________

8600 boxes?　______________

10 000 boxes?　______________

You can check any subtraction by changing the sum into an addition and seeing if you get the number you started with.

336 − 52 = 284   check   284 + 52 = 336

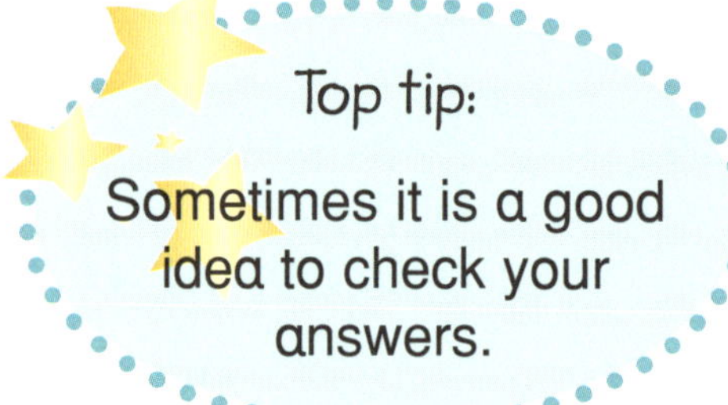

Mary did some subtractions.
Use an addition to check whether she got them right.
Put a tick by the ones she got right and a cross by the ones she got wrong.

425 − 38 = 387 ______

347 − 85 = 262 ______

235 − 57 = 176 ______

118 − 63 =   45 ______

531 − 143 = 388 ______

You can also use multiplication to check divisions:

120 ÷ 4 = 30
check   30 × 4 = 120

Jacob did some divisions.
Check his answers by doing a multiplication. Be careful – he got some wrong!

Tick the right divisions and put a cross by the wrong ones.

350 ÷ 5 = 70 ______

84 ÷ 4 = 22 ______

156 ÷ 3 = 52 ______

164 ÷ 4 = 41 ______

225 ÷ 5 = 44 ______

Another way to check your calculations is to make an estimate to see if you are about right.

38 + 47 = 85	estimate	40 + 50 = 90	about right
713 − 68 = 145	estimate	700 − 70 = 630	must be wrong
38 x 9 = 214	estimate	40 x 10 = 400	must be wrong
963 − 9 = 954	estimate	1000 − 10 = 900	about right

Use an estimate to check these calculations and put a cross by the ones you think are wrong:

67 + 198 = 355 ______

651 − 49 = 202 ______

52 x 11 = 572 ______

486 − 9 = 540 ______

Show your workings here:

Top tip:

If you add even numbers together, the answer is always even.

16 + 18 + 12 = 46
even   even   even   even

Put a cross by the sums you think are wrong:

8 + 12 + 18 = 38 ______   14 + 24 + 32 + 16 = 86 ______

24 + 30 + 16 = 83 ______   246 + 348 = 594 ______

56 + 38 = 121 ______   356 + 462 = 889 ______

This shape has a line of symmetry marked down the middle.

A line of symmetry is like a mirror image line.

One side of the line of symmetry is an exact mirror image of the other.

Complete these shapes where the line of symmetry is marked:

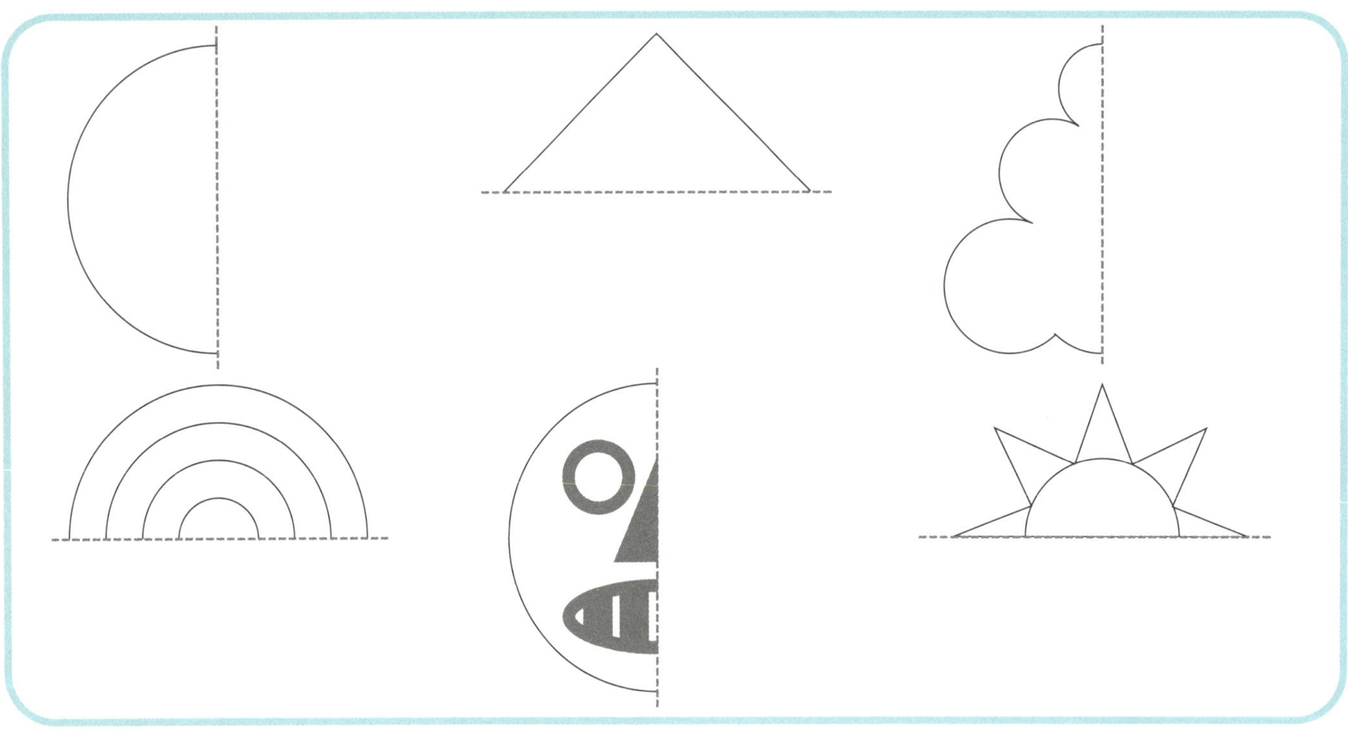

Now mark the line of symmetry on these shapes:

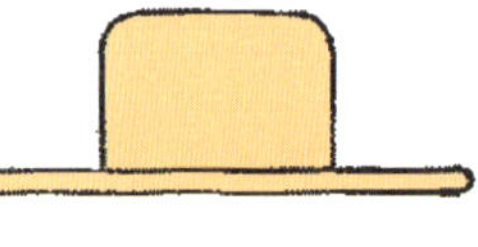
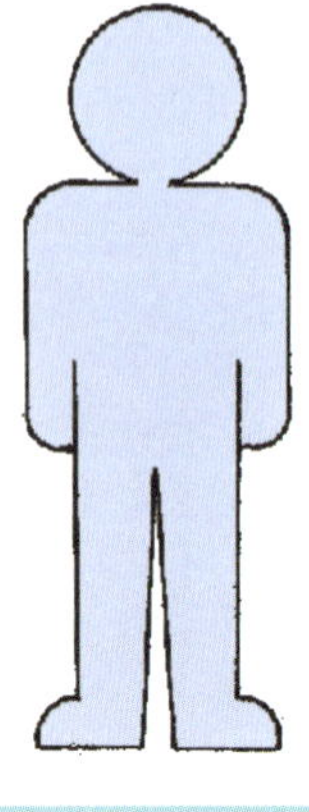

Lines of Symmetry

Many shapes have more than one line of symmetry. This butterfly has two.

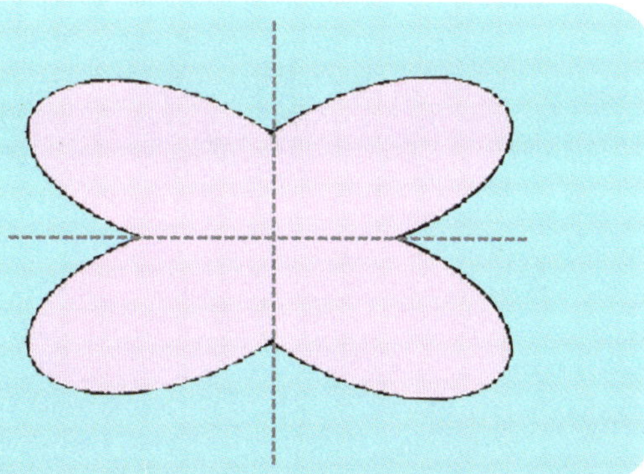

Complete these shapes so they each have more than one line of symmetry. The lines of symmetry are marked on the pictures.

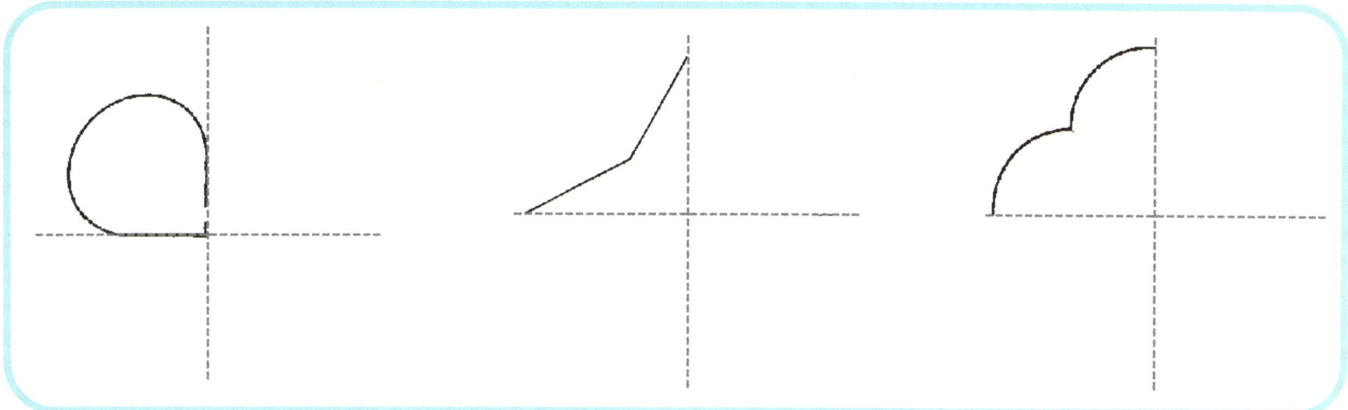

How many lines of symmetry does each shape have?

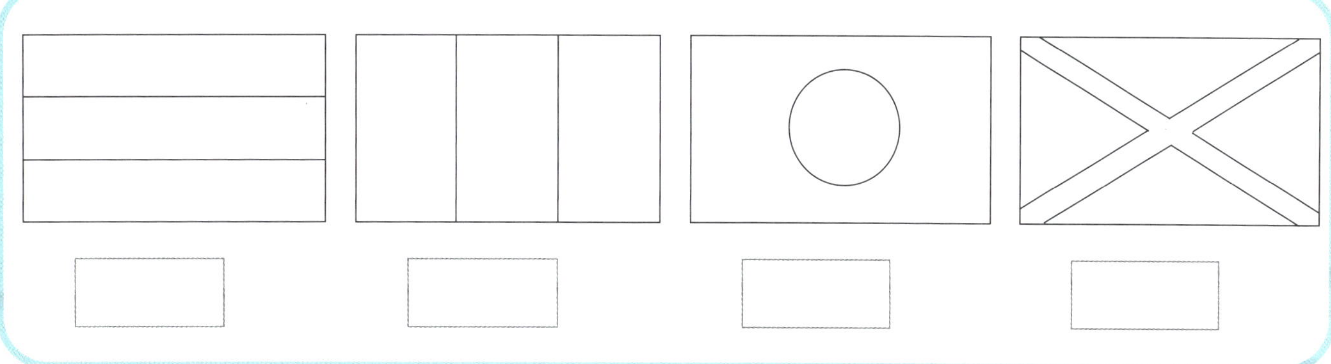

An angle is the space between two lines. Put these angles in the correct order. Start with the smallest.

Top tip:
Use the corner of a piece of paper to help you, or trace the angles and compare them on paper.

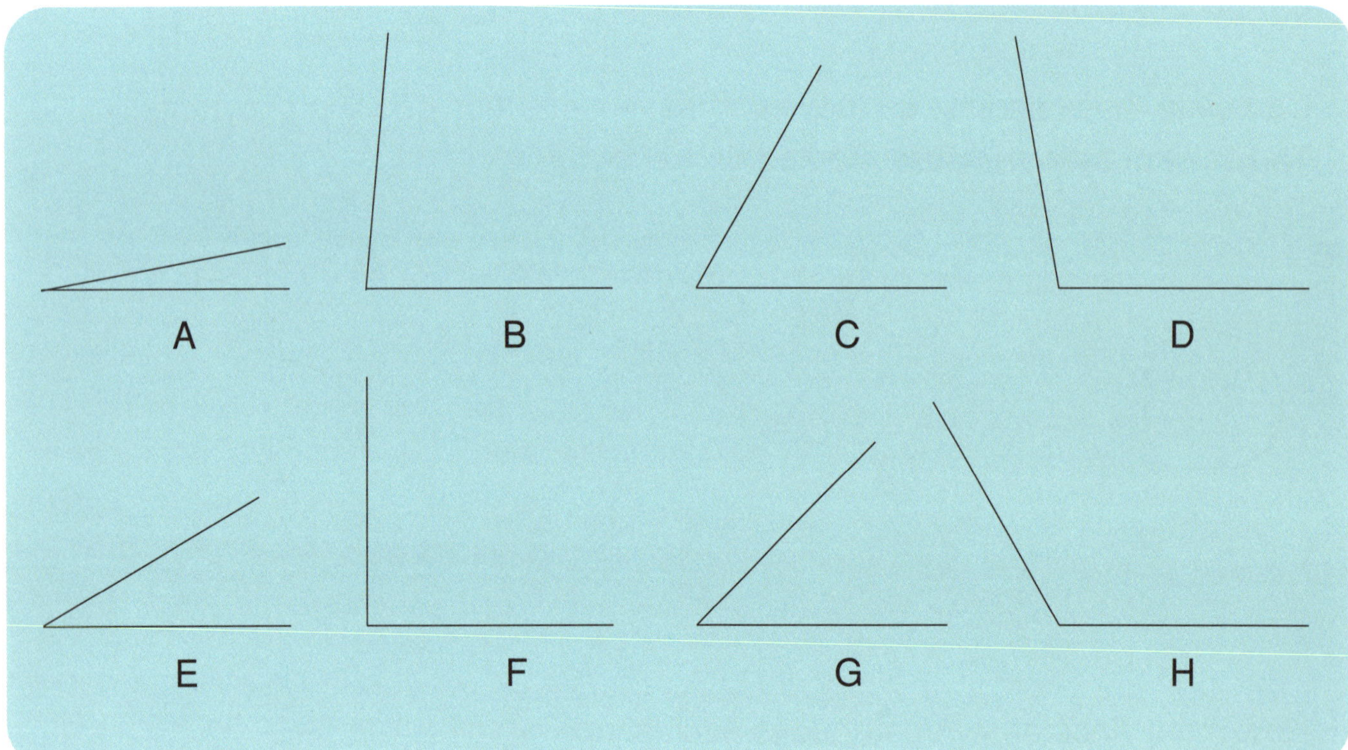

The correct order is:

____

A right angle is a quarter turn. This is a right angle:
This angle is bigger than a right angle:
This angle is smaller than a right angle:

Angles and shapes

For each shape, answer these questions:

1. What is its name?
2. How many sides does it have?
3. How many right angles does it have?
4. How many angles are larger than a right angle?
5. How many angles are smaller than a right angle?
6. How many vertices are there?

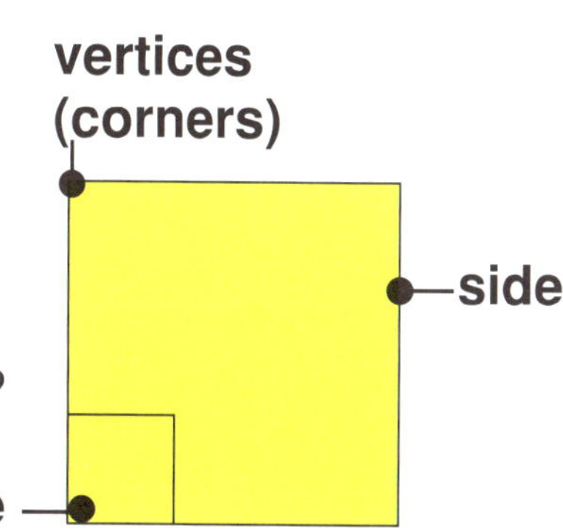

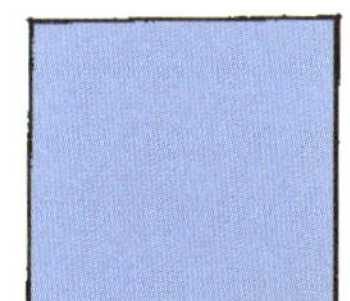

1.____________________
2.__________ 3.__________
4.__________ 5.__________ 6.__________

1.____________________
2.__________ 3.__________
4.__________ 5.__________ 6.__________

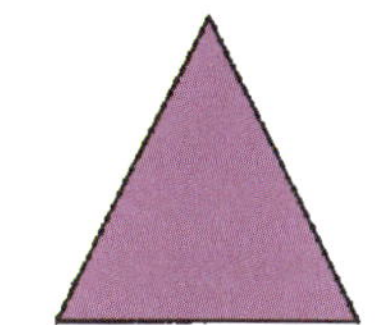

1.____________________
2.__________ 3.__________
4.__________ 5.__________ 6.__________

1.____________________
2.__________ 3.__________
4.__________ 5.__________ 6.__________

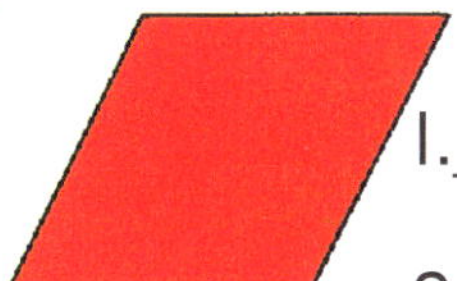

1.____________________
2.__________ 3.__________
4.__________ 5.__________ 6.__________

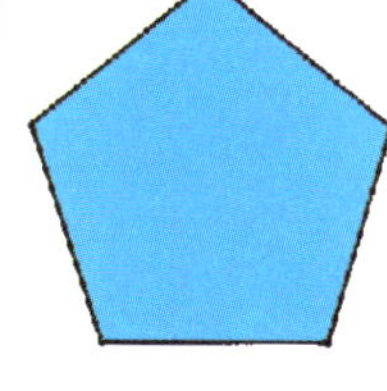

1.____________________
2.__________ 3.__________
4.__________ 5.__________ 6.__________

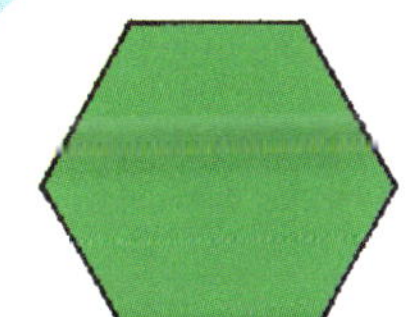

1.____________________
2.__________ 3.__________
4.__________ 5.__________ 6.__________

1.____________________
2.__________ 3.__________
4.__________ 5.__________ 6.__________

Write the letter of each shape alongside
the correct name in the table below.

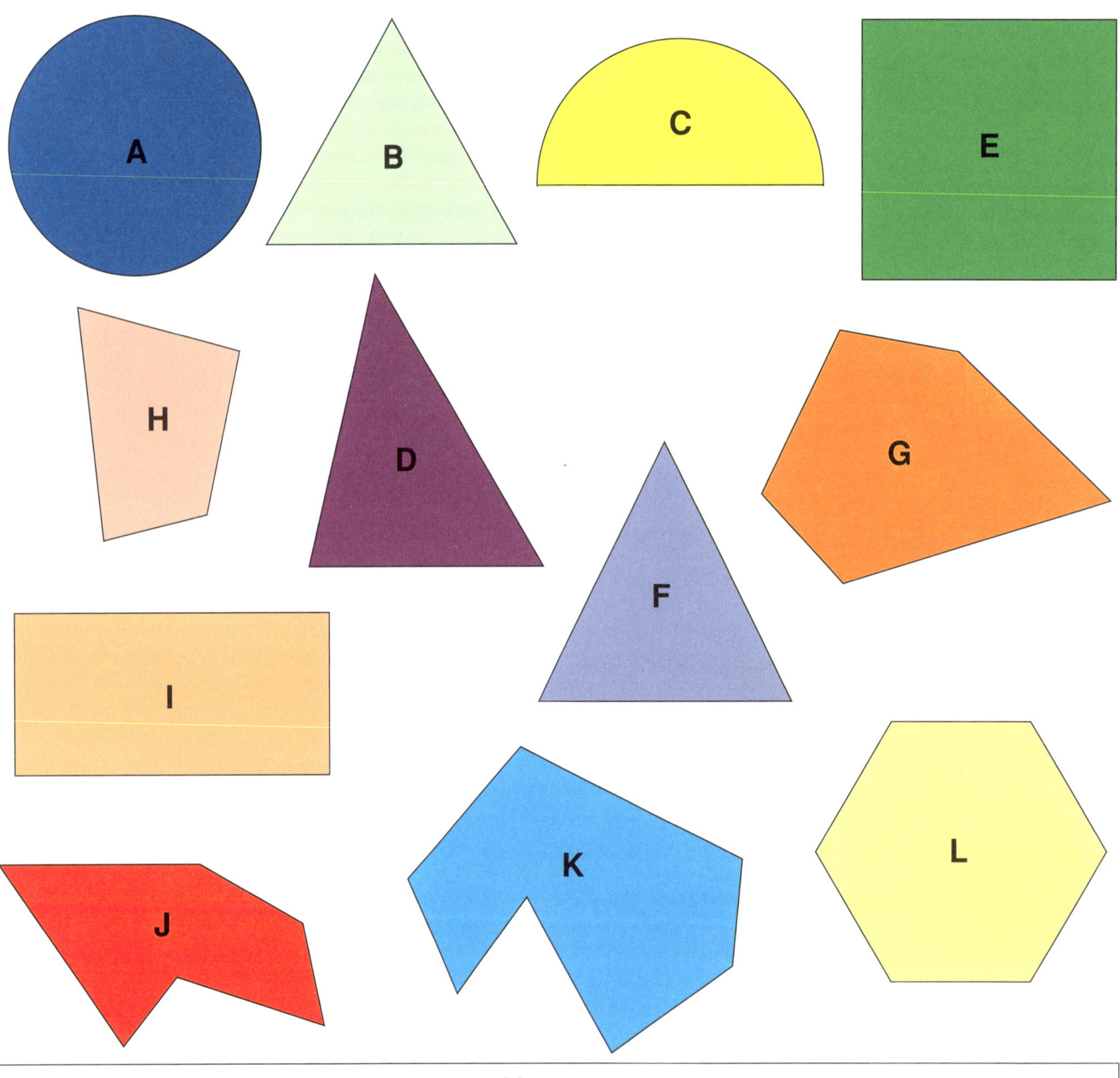

Names							
isosceles triangle		rectangle		circle		hexagon	
triangle		semi-circle		regular hexagon		square	
equilateral triangle		pentagon		quadrilateral		heptagon	

Fill in the number of faces, edges
and vertices for each of the shapes below.

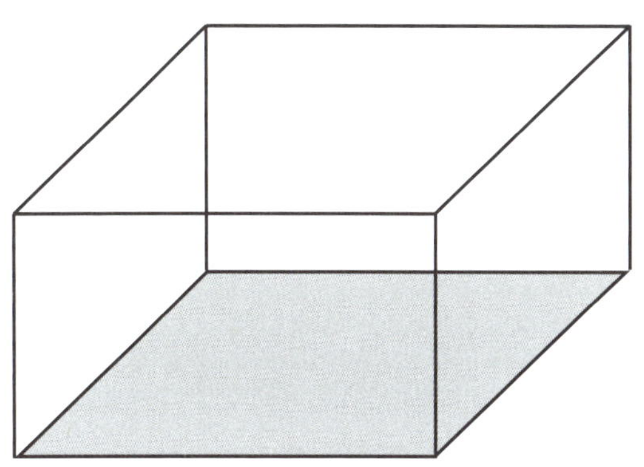

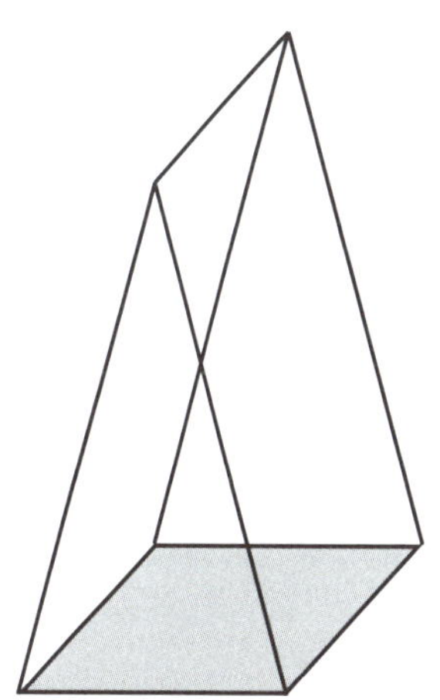

Cuboid

Faces ___________________________

Edges ___________________________

Vertices ___________________________

Triangular Prism

Faces ___________________________

Edges ___________________________

Vertices ___________________________

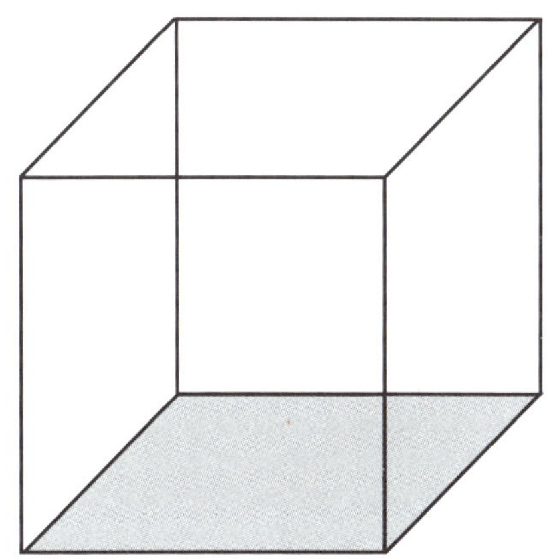

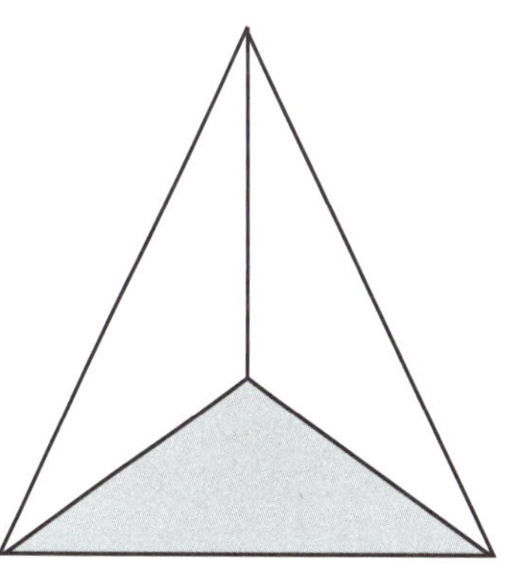

Cube

Faces ___________________________

Edges ___________________________

Vertices ___________________________

Tetrahedron

Faces ___________________________

Edges ___________________________

Vertices ___________________________

The perimeter is the total distance around a shape.

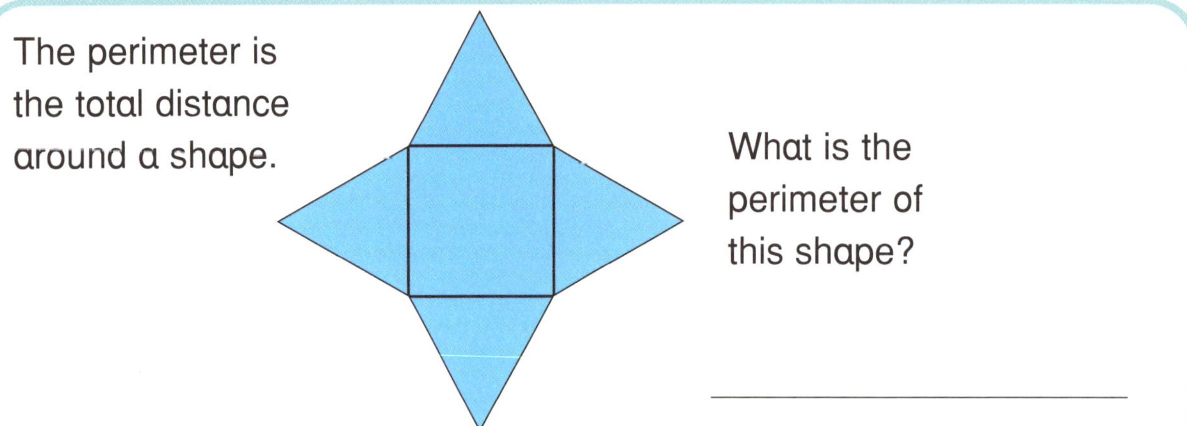

What is the perimeter of this shape?

____

A regular octagon has sides that measure 3cm each.

What is its perimeter? _______________________

Which is bigger: a hexagon where each side measures 3cm,

or a square where side measures 4cm? _______________________

Draw four shapes on the grid below:

perimeter = 8cm   perimeter = 12cm
perimeter = 4cm   perimeter = 10cm

To calculate the area of a shape we multiply its length by its breadth.

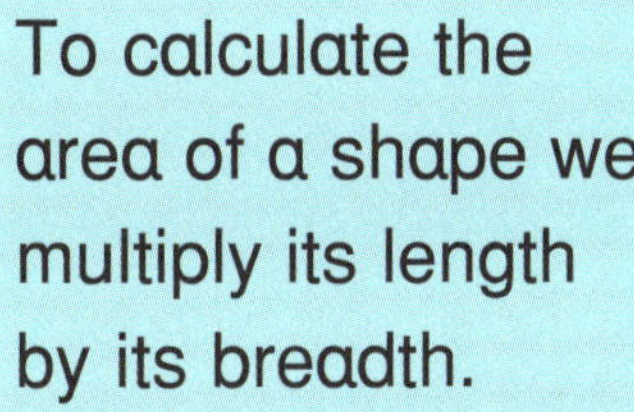

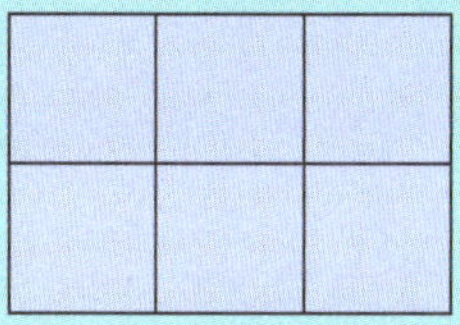

3 centimetre squares x 2 centimetre squares = 6 centimetre squares.

We write this as 6cm^2.

Measure the length and breadth of each shape. Then calculate the area of each shape.

A

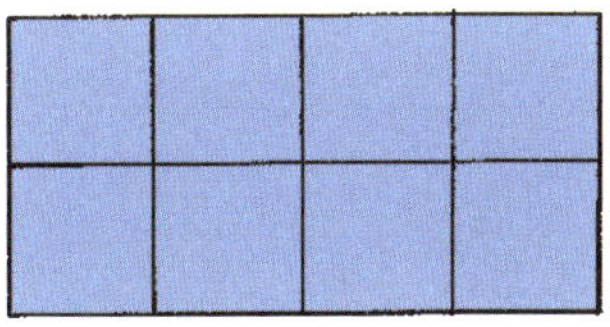

B

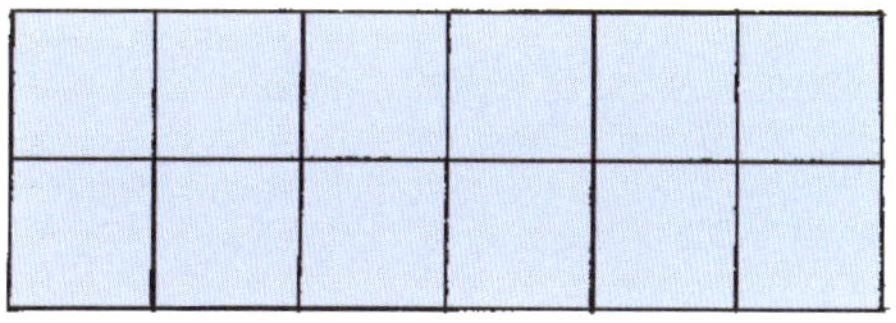

____

____

C

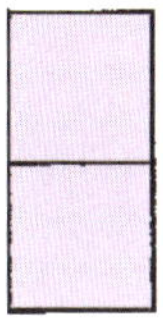

____

E

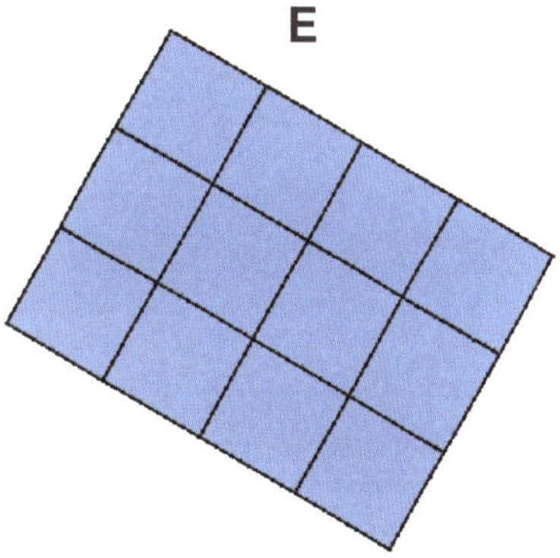

D

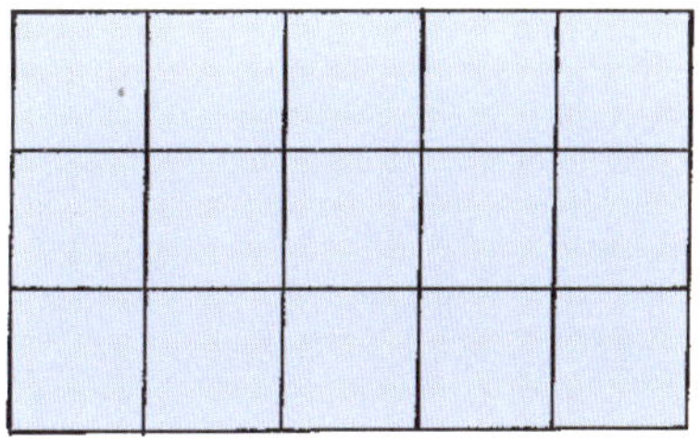

____

____

F

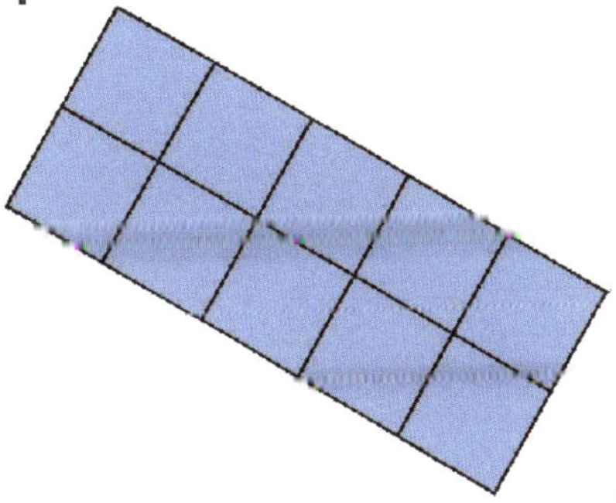

G

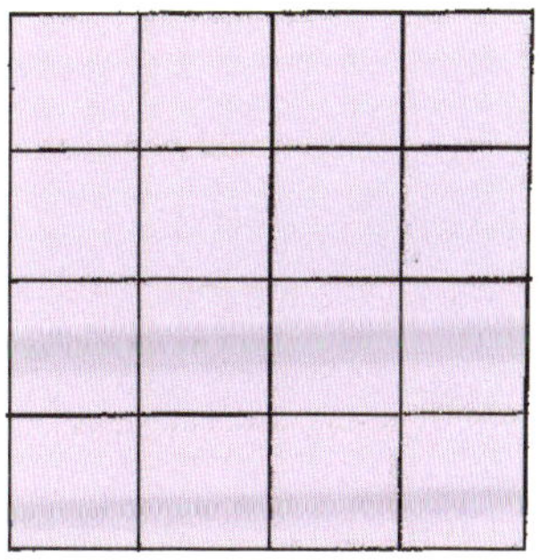

____

____

More perimeter and area

Measure and calculate the perimeter and area of these rectangles.

A

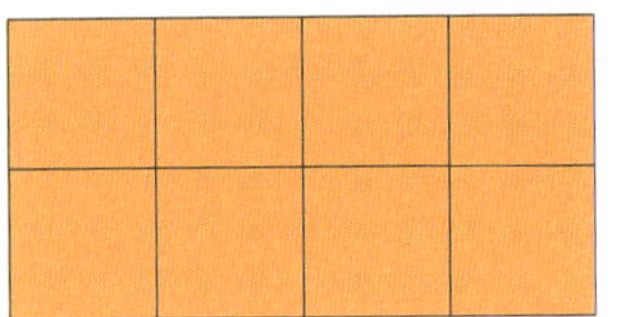

perimeter = ___________________

area   = ___________________

B

perimeter = ___________________

area   = ___________________

C

perimeter = ___________________

area   = ___________________

D

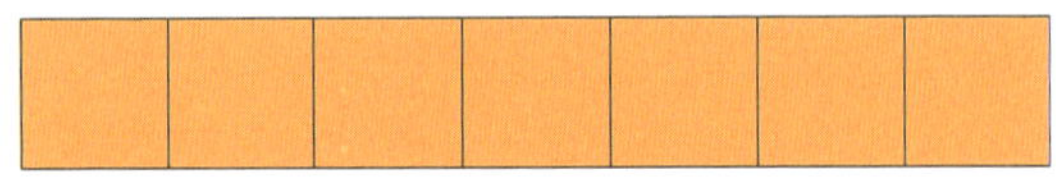

perimeter = ___________________

area   = ___________________

E

perimeter = ___________________

area   = ___________________

F

perimeter = ___________________

area   = ___________________

More perimeter and area

Measure and calculate the perimeter and area of these shapes.

A

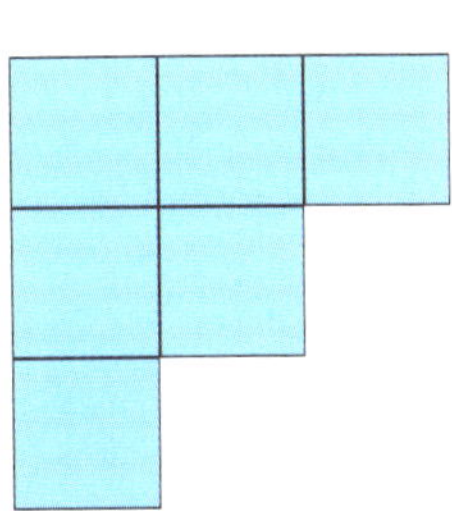

perimeter = _______________________

area = _______________________

B

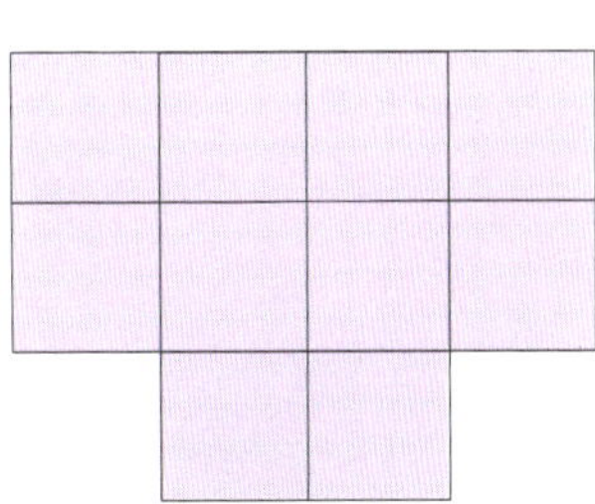

perimeter = _______________________

area = _______________________

C

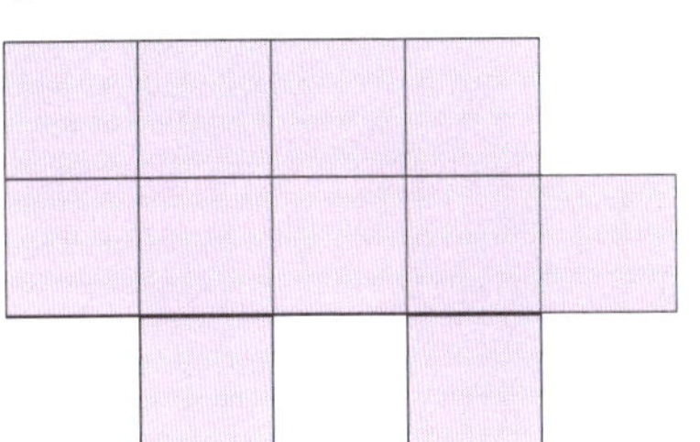

perimeter = _______________________

area = _______________________

D

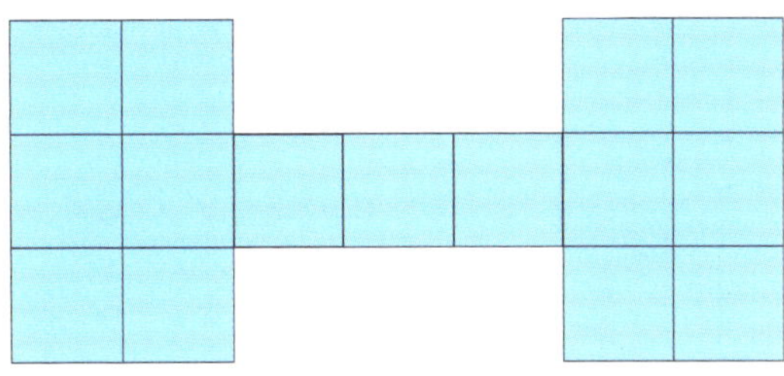

perimeter = _______________________

area = _______________________

E

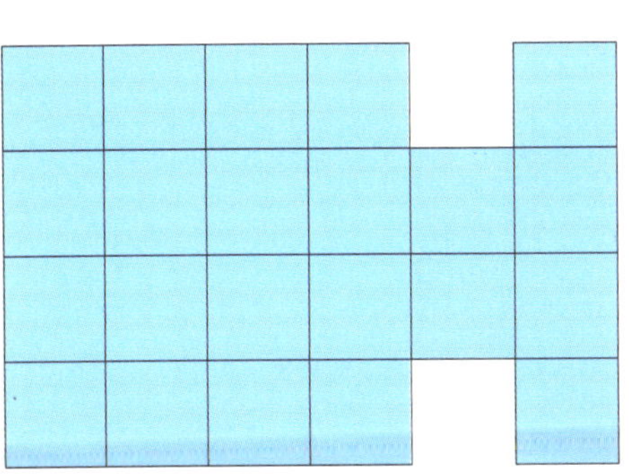

perimeter = _______________________

area = _______________________

F

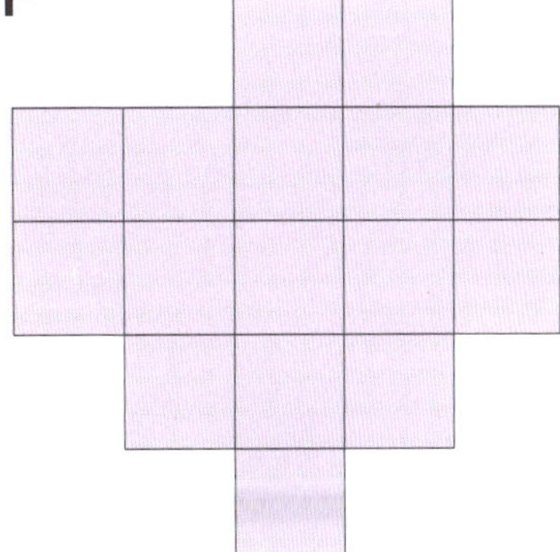

perimeter = _______________________

area = _______________________

Calculating volume

We calculate the volume of an object by multiplying its length by its height and then by its width.

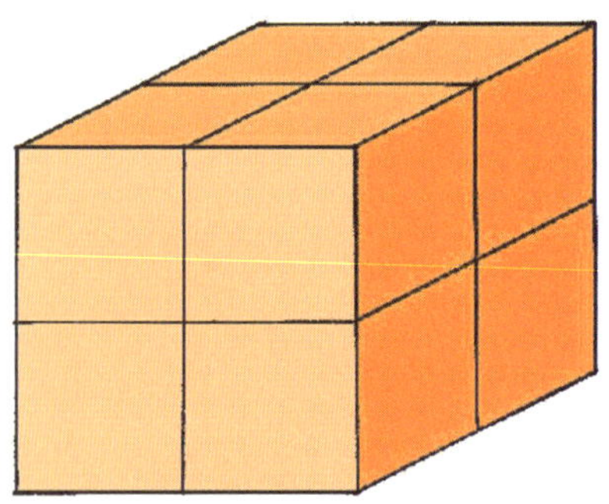

What is the volume of this object? Volume is noted with ^{3} after the unit of measurement

____

This shape is 2cm long, 2cm high and 2cm wide.
2cm x 2cm x 2cm = $8cm^3$

Calculate the volume of these objects.
They are not drawn to scale.

A

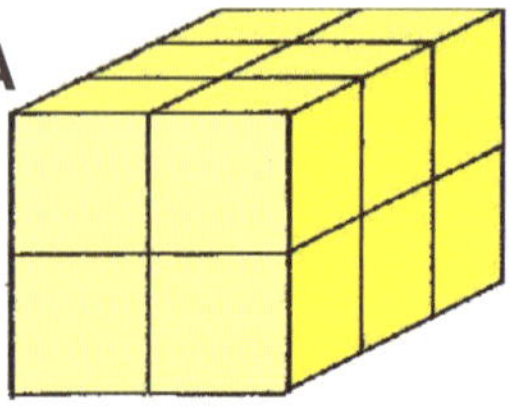

2cm x 2cm x 3cm =

____________ cm^3

D

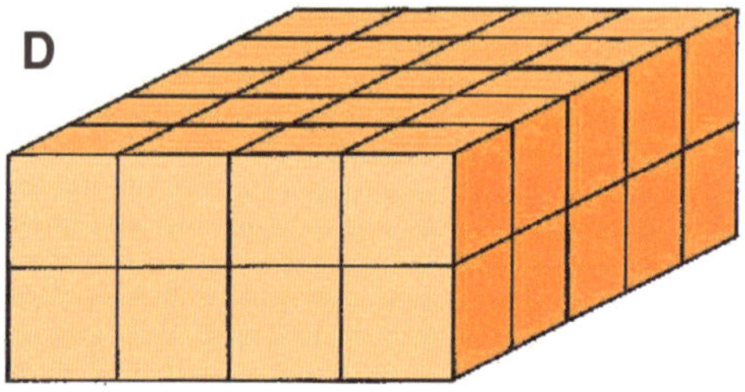

4cm x 2cm x 5cm =

____________ cm^3

B

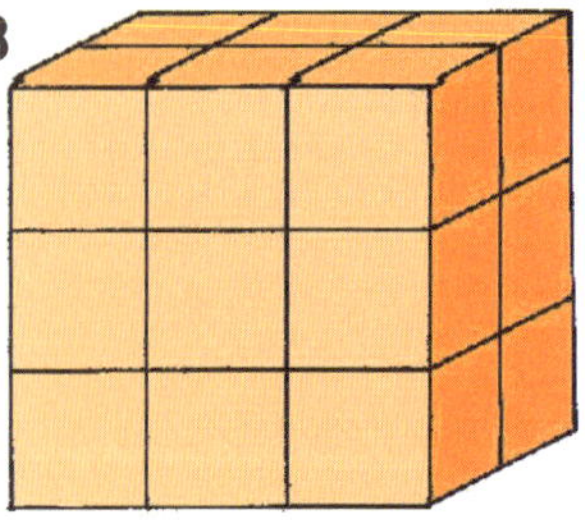

3cm x 3cm x 2cm =

____________ cm^3

E

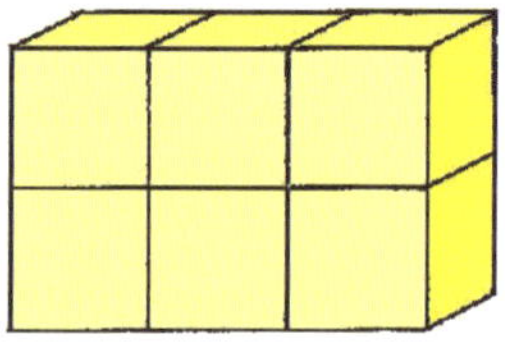

3cm x 2cm x 1cm =

____________ cm^3

C

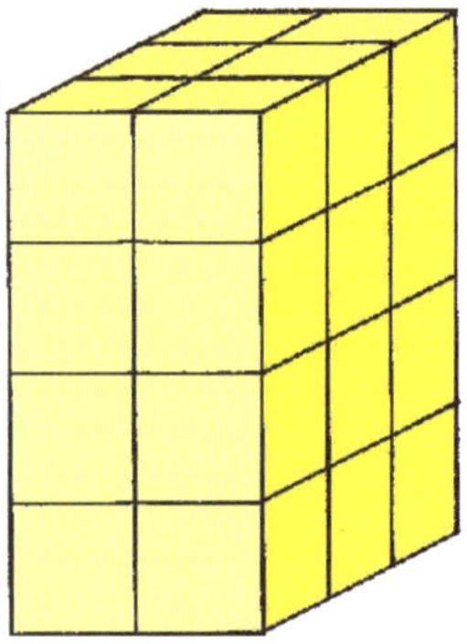

2cm x 4cm x 3cm =

____________ cm^3

F

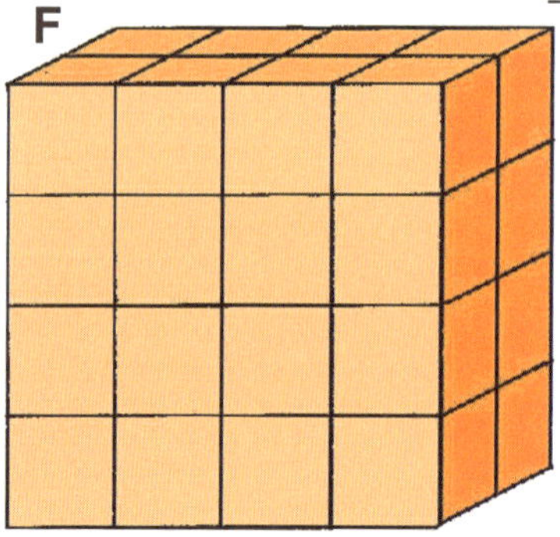

4cm x 4cm x 2cm =

____________ cm^3

Calculating volume

This cube has a volume of Icm³.

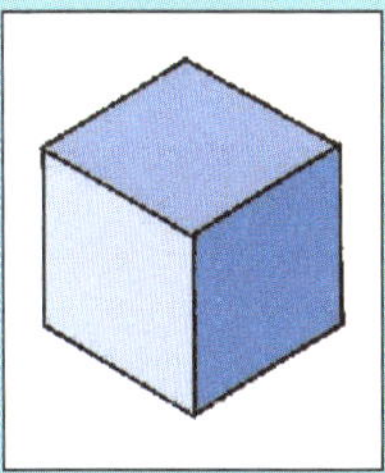

What is the volume of this shape?

A

_________________________ cm³

Work out the volumes of these irregular shapes.
They are all made from centimetre cubes.

B

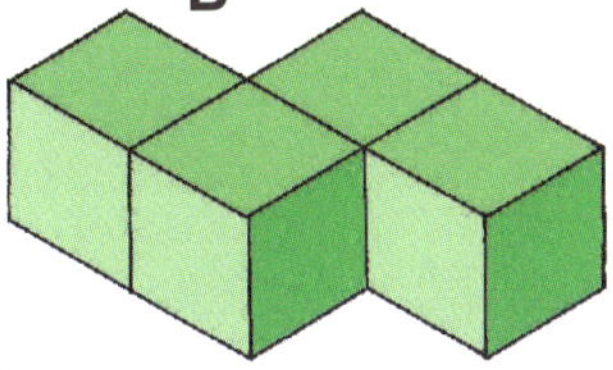

____

C

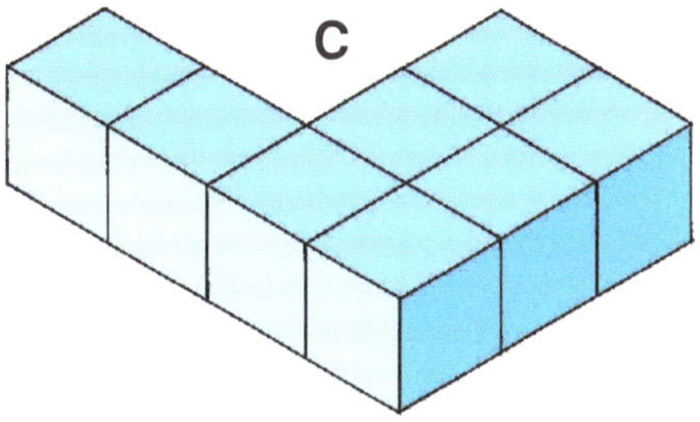

____

D

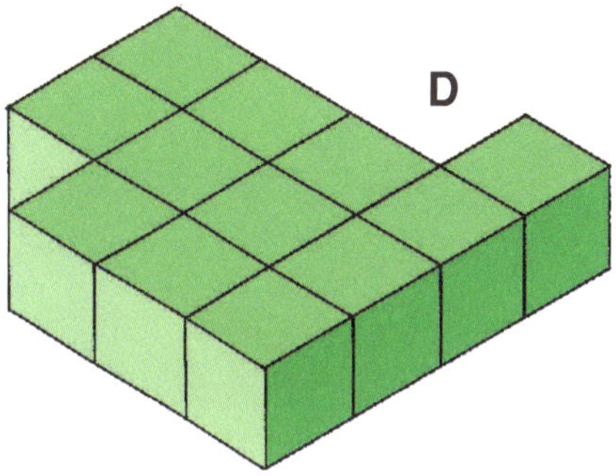

____

E

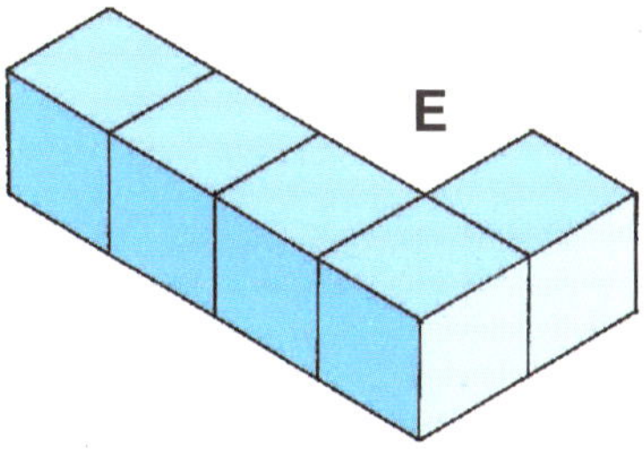

____

F

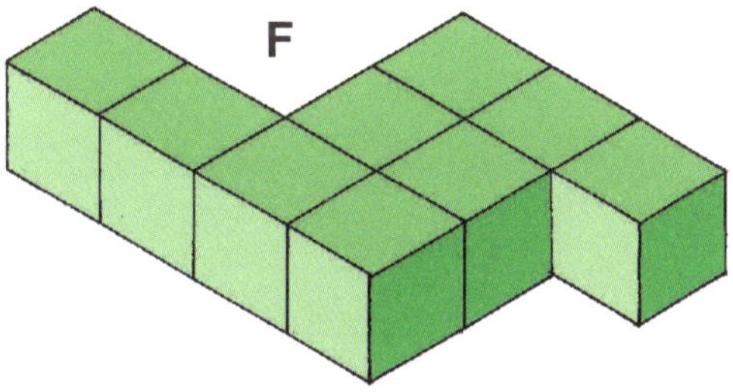

____

G

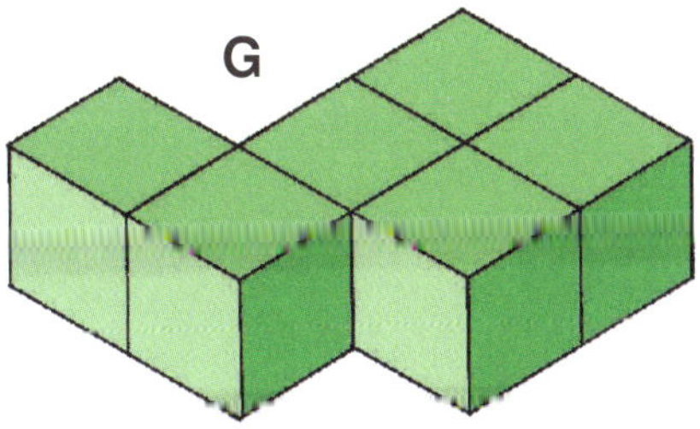

____

H

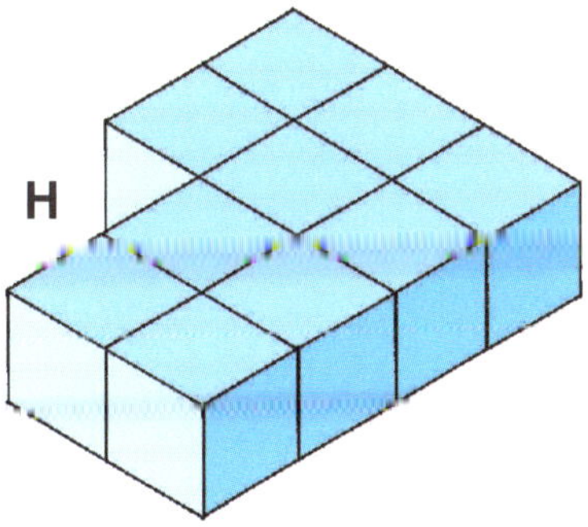

____

I

Choose from the list below, to show which instrument
and unit you would use to measure each object.

Object	Instrument	Unit
	measuring jug	ml
	ruler	cm
	scales	g
	tape measure	m
	foot measure	

I

Coffee in a mug _______________   _______________

2

Length of a foot _______________   _______________

3

Weight of an apple _______________   _______________

4

Length of a scarf _______________   _______________

Top tip:

Remember to use metric units, i.e. kilometres not miles.

Write down the units you would use to measure:

The distance from Liverpool to Manchester _______________________

The height of a giraffe _______________________

The weight of a baby _______________________

The weight of a potato _______________________

The fizzy orange drink in a can _______________________

The weight of a packet of crisps _______________________

The length of a pencil _______________________

The thickness of a book _______________________

The amount of lemonade in a large bottle _______________________

The thickness of a coin _______________________

How many centimetres are there in a metre? ____________

10cm is $\frac{1}{10}$ of a metre. We can write $\frac{1}{10}$ of a metre like this: 0.10m.

How many centimetres are there in half a metre? ____________

We can write this as 0.50m.

How many centimetres are there in these metre measurements?

0.75m   0.38m   1.34m   1.54m   0.98m

__________   __________   __________   __________   __________

We can write 132cm as 1.32m.
Write out these centimetre measurements in metres:

142cm   154cm   198cm   98cm   134cm

__________   __________   __________   __________   __________

Length

Colour in the lengths that are equal with the same colour.

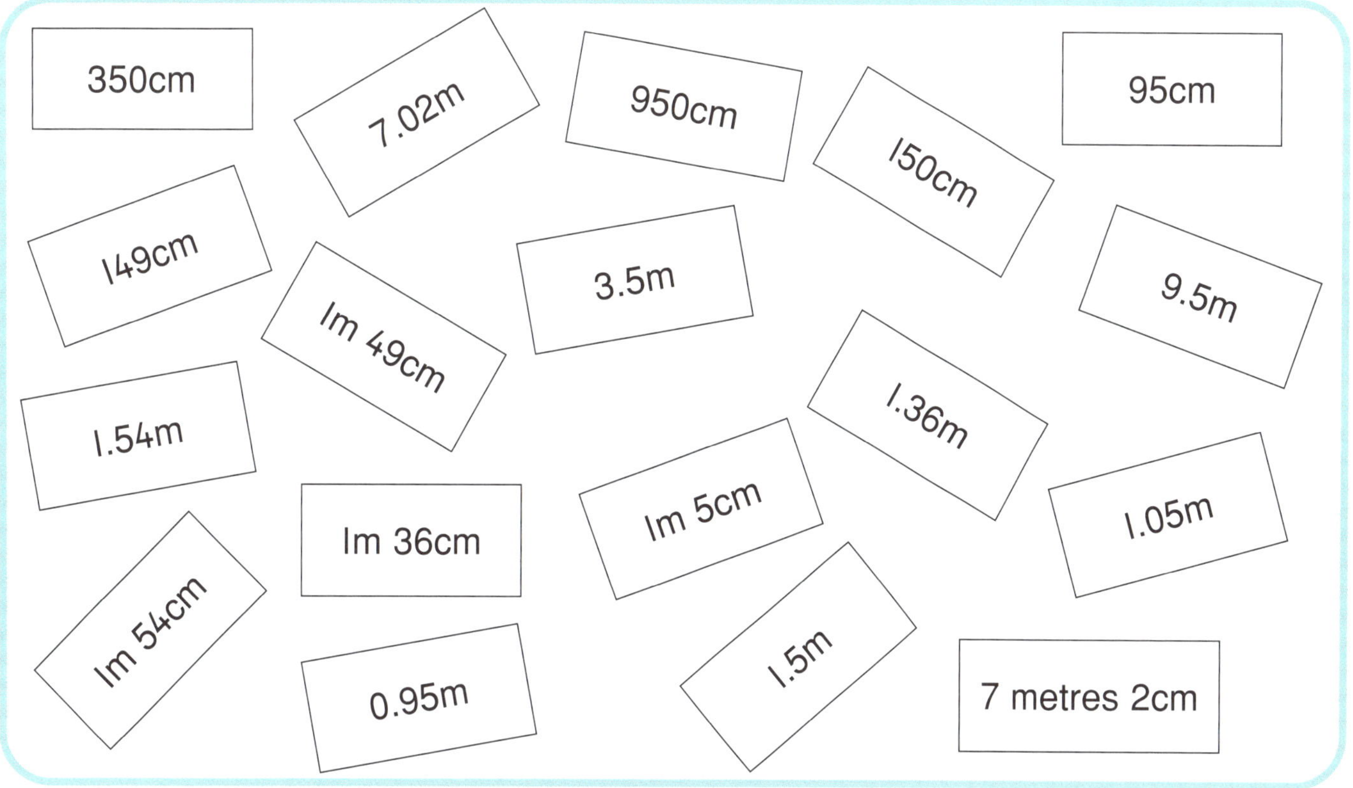

Now write each pair next to each other.

How much liquid is there in each measuring cylinder?

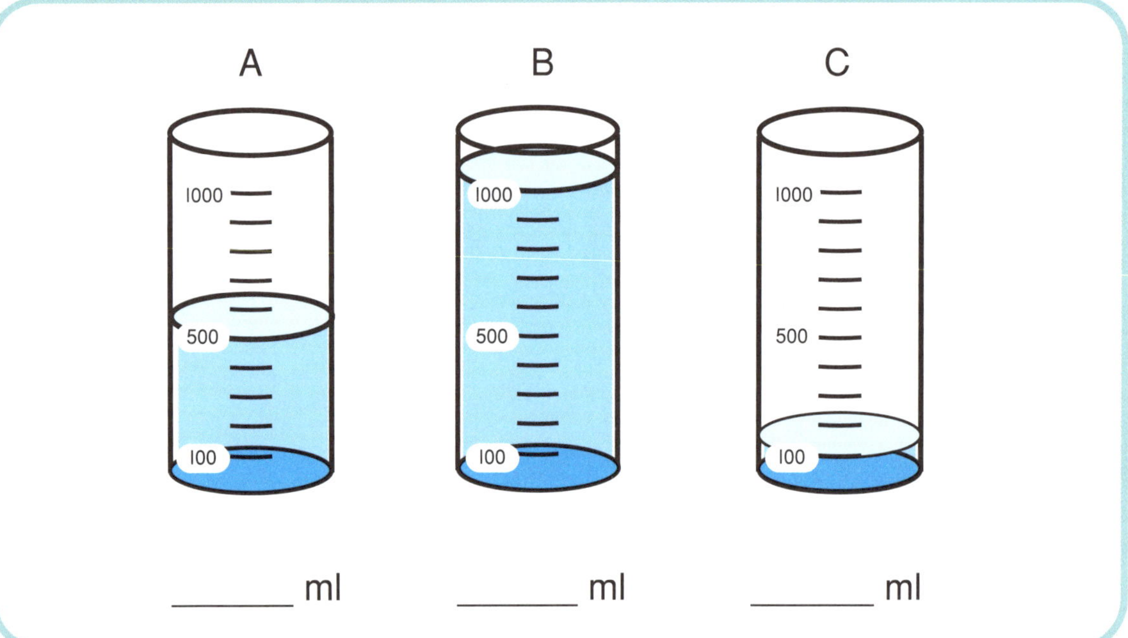

Which cylinder has the greatest amount of liquid? ___________

Which cylinder has the least amount of liquid? ___________

Look at the cylinders below carefully.
How much liquid does each cylinder contain?

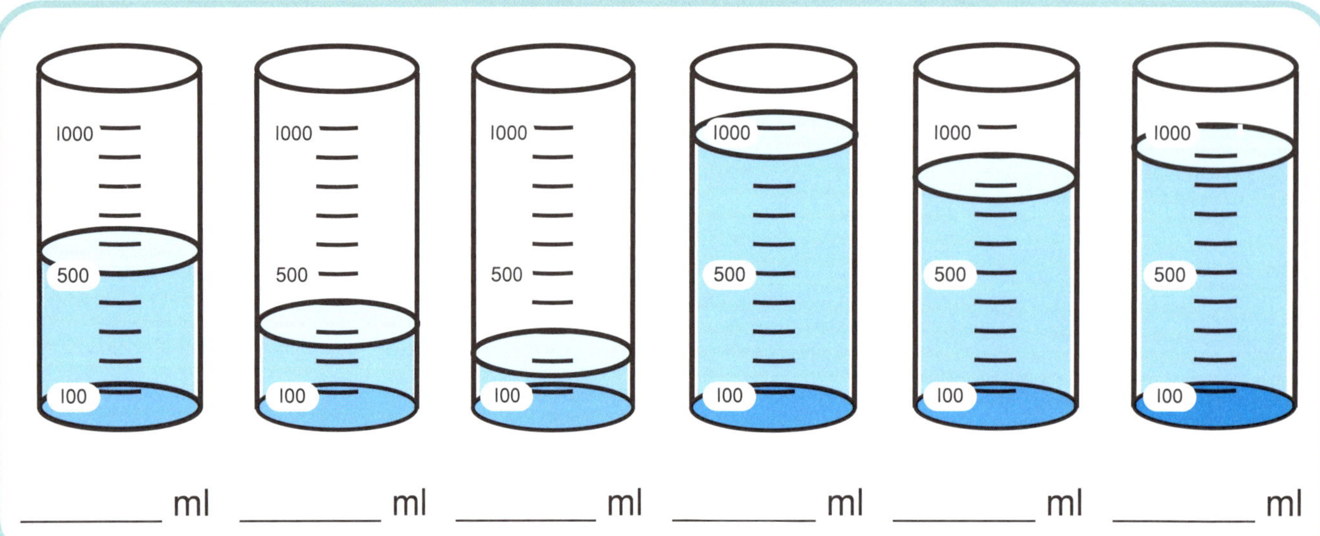

Measuring capacity and mass

How much does each parcel weigh?

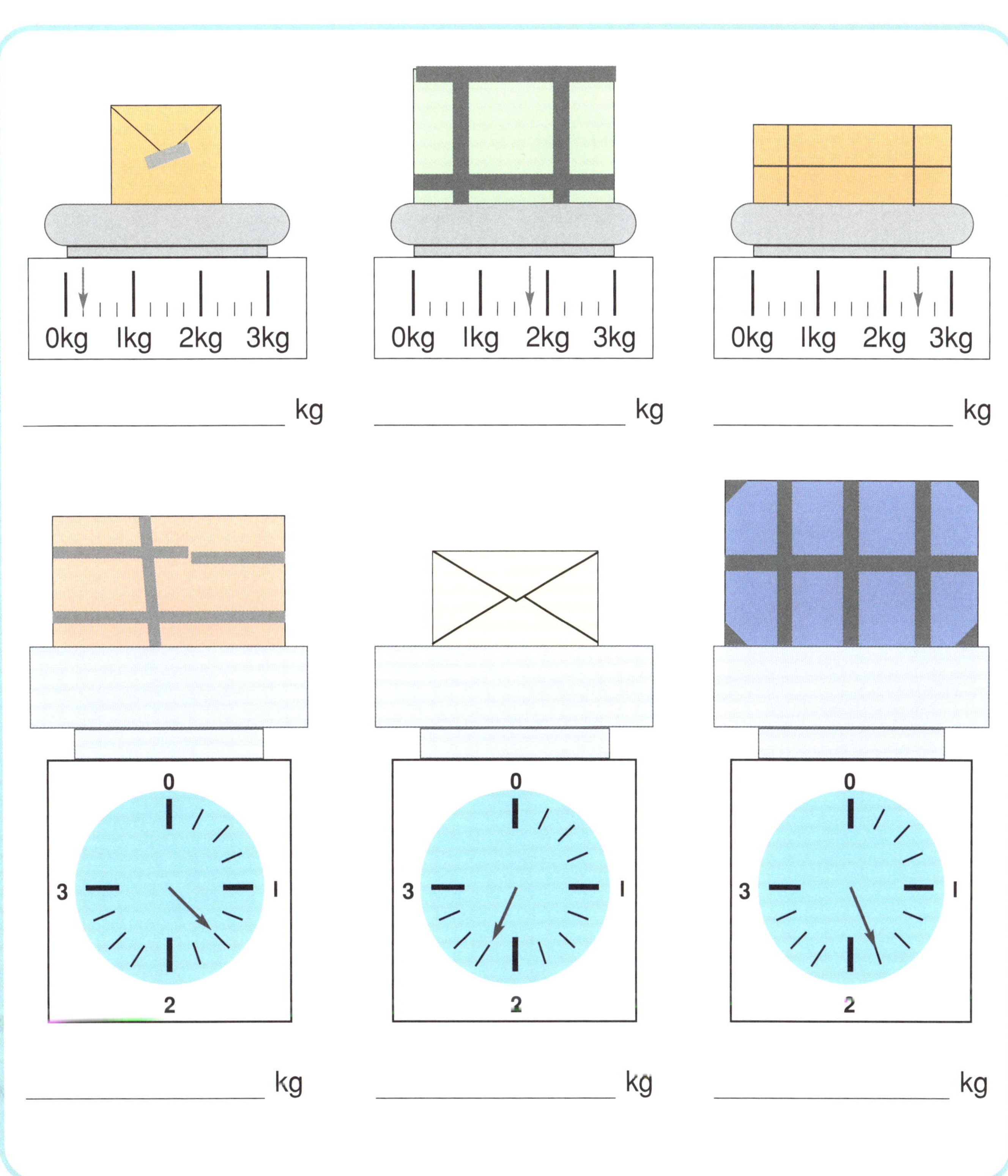

Read the scales and write the answers in each box.

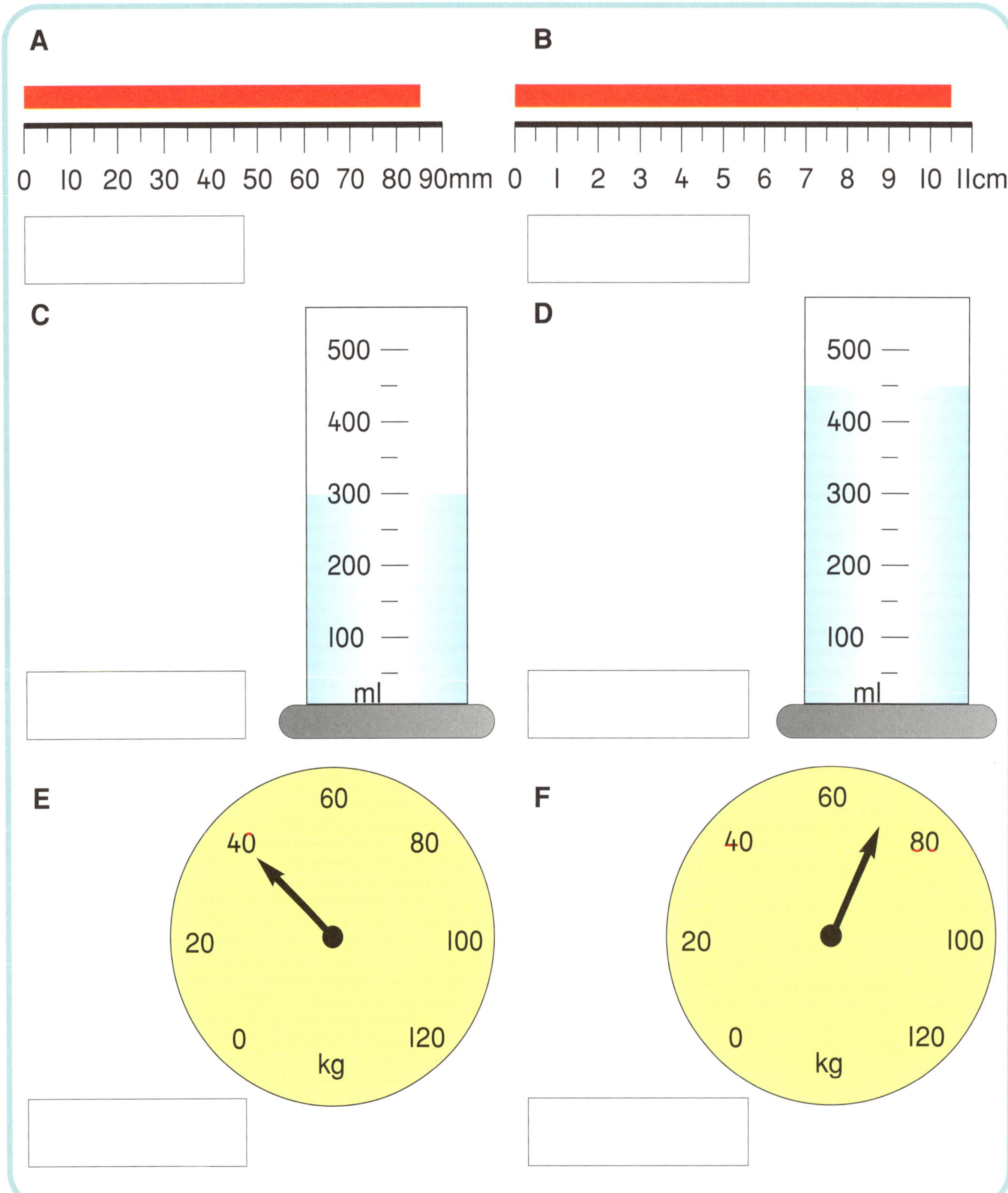

Reading scales

Round each measurement to the nearest unit.

A

Round to the nearest 10cm	
342cm	________________cm
152cm	________________cm
428cm	________________cm
337cm	________________cm

B

Round to the nearest 10cm	
53cm	________________cm
7cm	________________cm
603cm	________________cm
598cm	________________cm

C

Round to the nearest 100 grams	
238g	________________g
1178g	________________g
4640g	________________g
5788g	________________g

D

Round to the nearest 100 grams	
78g	________________g
29g	________________g
4287g	________________g
994g	________________g

Top tip:

When rounding to the nearest 10, we round up when the end digit is more than 5, and round down when it is less than 5.

When rounding to the nearest 100, we check to see if the end digits are more or less than 50.

Here is a piece of a calendar:

<table>
<tr><td colspan="7" align="center">NOVEMBER 2003</td></tr>
<tr><td>Sun</td><td>Mon</td><td>Tue</td><td>Wed</td><td>Thu</td><td>Fri</td><td>Sat</td></tr>
<tr><td></td><td>1</td><td>2</td><td>3</td><td>4</td><td>5</td><td>6</td></tr>
<tr><td>7</td><td>8</td><td>9</td><td>10</td><td>11</td><td>12</td><td>13</td></tr>
<tr><td>14</td><td>15</td><td>16</td><td>17</td><td>18</td><td>19</td><td>20</td></tr>
<tr><td>21</td><td>22</td><td>23</td><td>24</td><td>25</td><td>26</td><td>27</td></tr>
<tr><td>28</td><td>29</td><td>30</td><td></td><td></td><td></td><td></td></tr>
</table>

What day is the third of November? _______________________

What is the date a fortnight after that? _______________________

Today is the 17/11/03. Is the day before
it a week day or not? _______________________

What is the date a week after
the Monday 29th November? _______________________

If today is the last day of November, how many
days will I have to wait until Christmas day? _______________________

What date is three weeks before
Sunday 14 November? _______________________

Read this TV listing:

CHANNEL 1		Channel 2		FILM CHANNEL
				(new film every 2 hours)
4:00	ANIMAL SPECIAL	3:55	Ward 7	**Revenge of the Turtle** *(89 mins)*
4:25	CARTOON MYSTERY	4:35	News	________ ________
		4:45	Madcaps	**Haunted Castle IV** *(118 mins)*
4.50	HERO!	4:50	Junior Art	________ ________
____	MONSTER TRUCKS	____	Aussie Street	**Mad for Maths III** *(75 mins)*
				________ ________

Hero! lasts half an hour.
What time does *Monster Trucks* start? _______________ Now write it on the page.

Junior Art lasts for three quarters of an hour.
What time does *Aussie Street* begin? _______________ Now write it on the page.

How long does *Ward 7* last? _______________

How much longer does *Cartoon Mystery*
last than the *News*? _______________

Next week there is a two-hour episode of *Animal Special*.
How many more minutes is this than the normal programme? _______________

A film begins every two hours on the film channel.
The films start at 4:00.
Write the time each film starts and finishes on the listing at the top of the page.

Reflecting shapes

Reflect the shape in the dotted line.

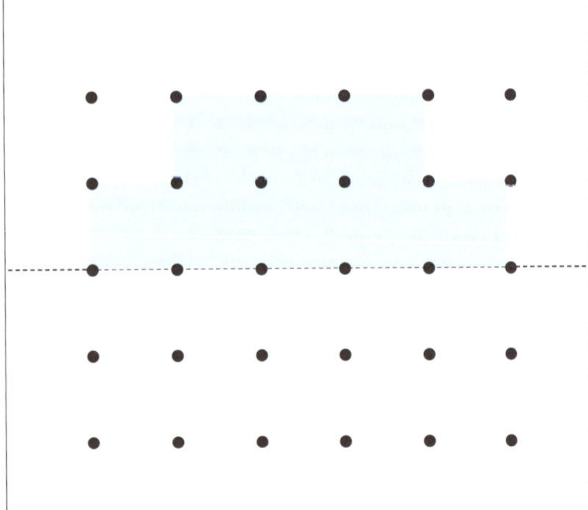

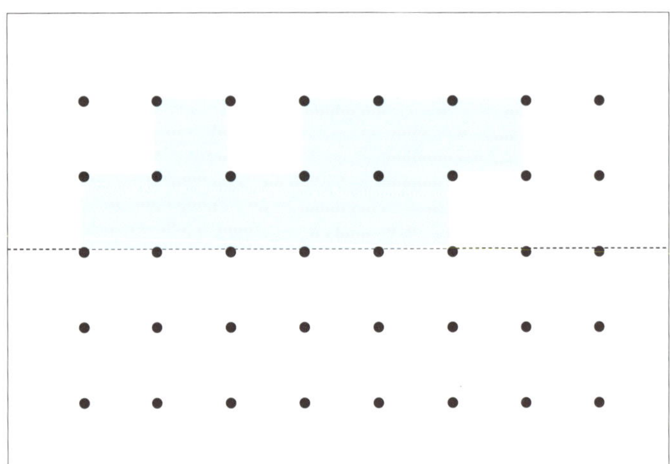

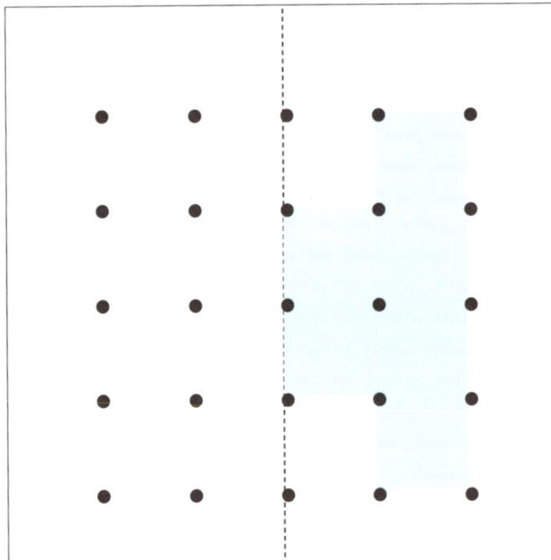

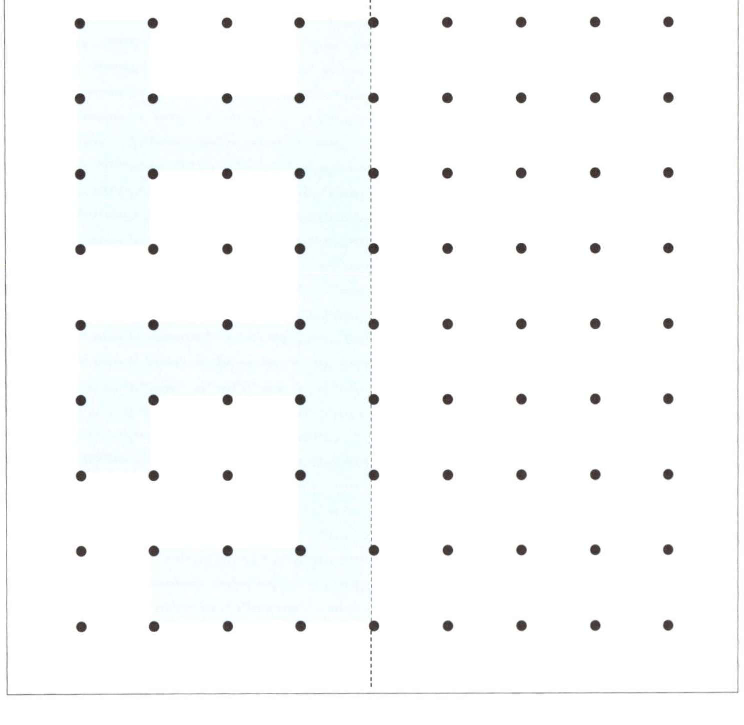

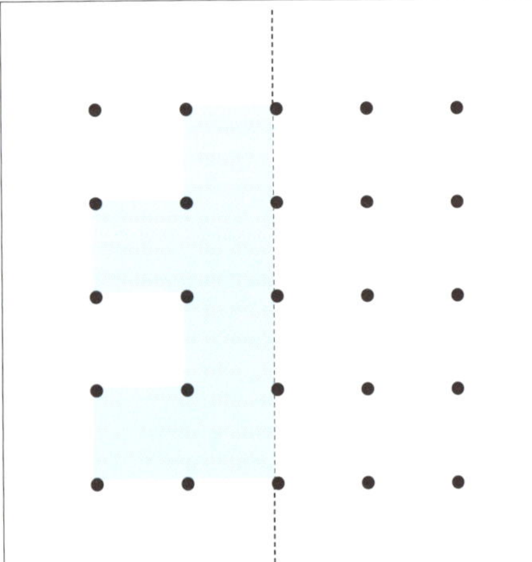

Reflecting shapes

Now reflect each of these shapes in the dotted line.

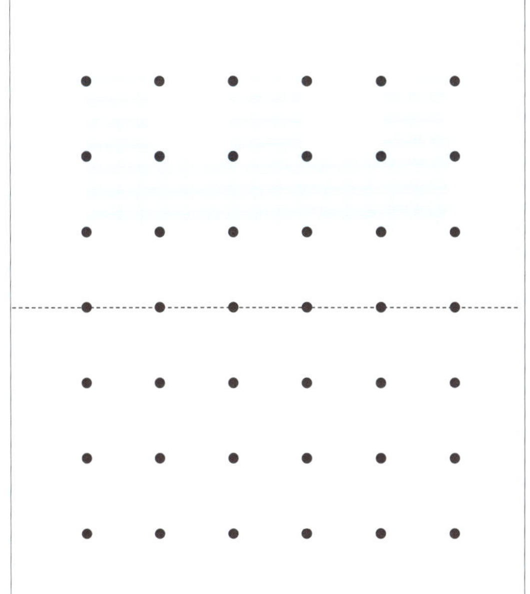

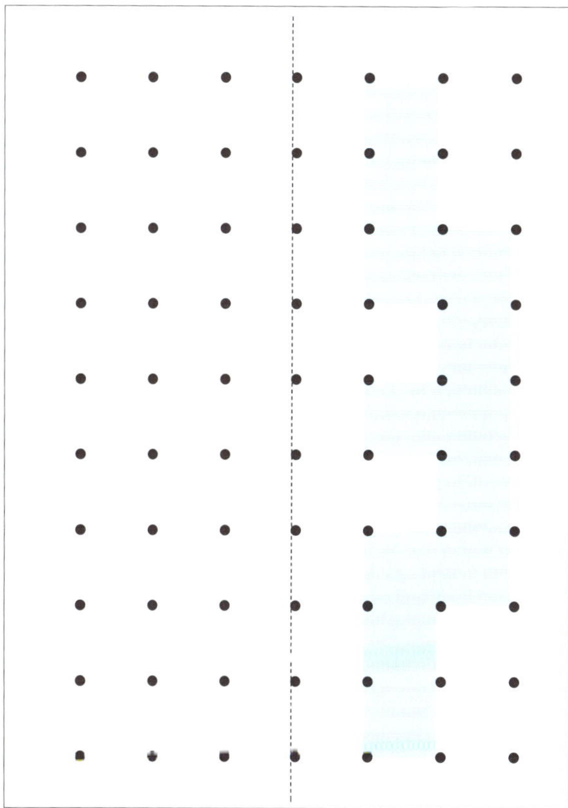

How much of each shape is coloured in?
Use the words and fractions at the bottom of the page to fill in the spaces under each shape.

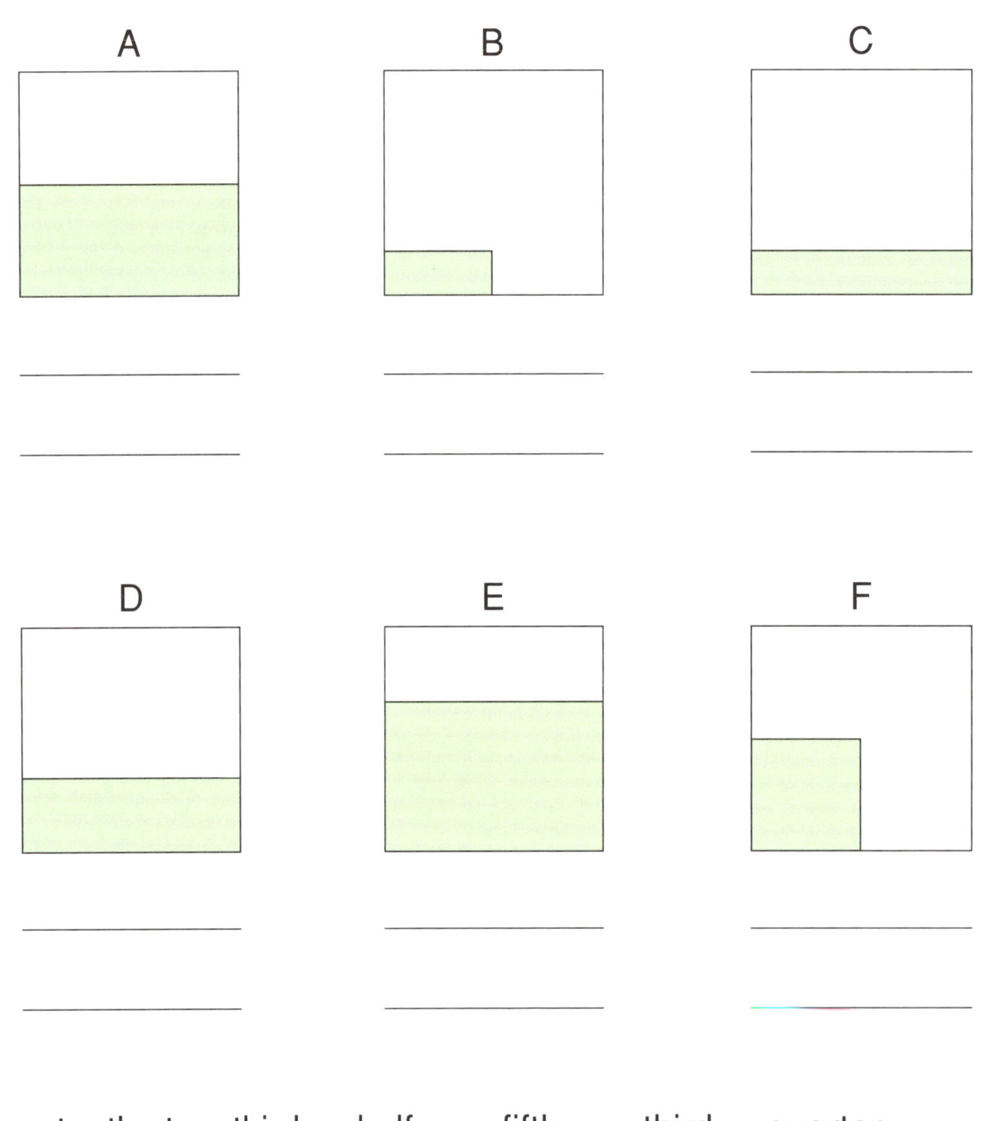

$$\frac{1}{2} \qquad \frac{1}{10} \qquad \frac{1}{5} \qquad \frac{1}{3} \qquad \frac{2}{3} \qquad \frac{1}{4}$$

Colour in each shape to match the amount written underneath.

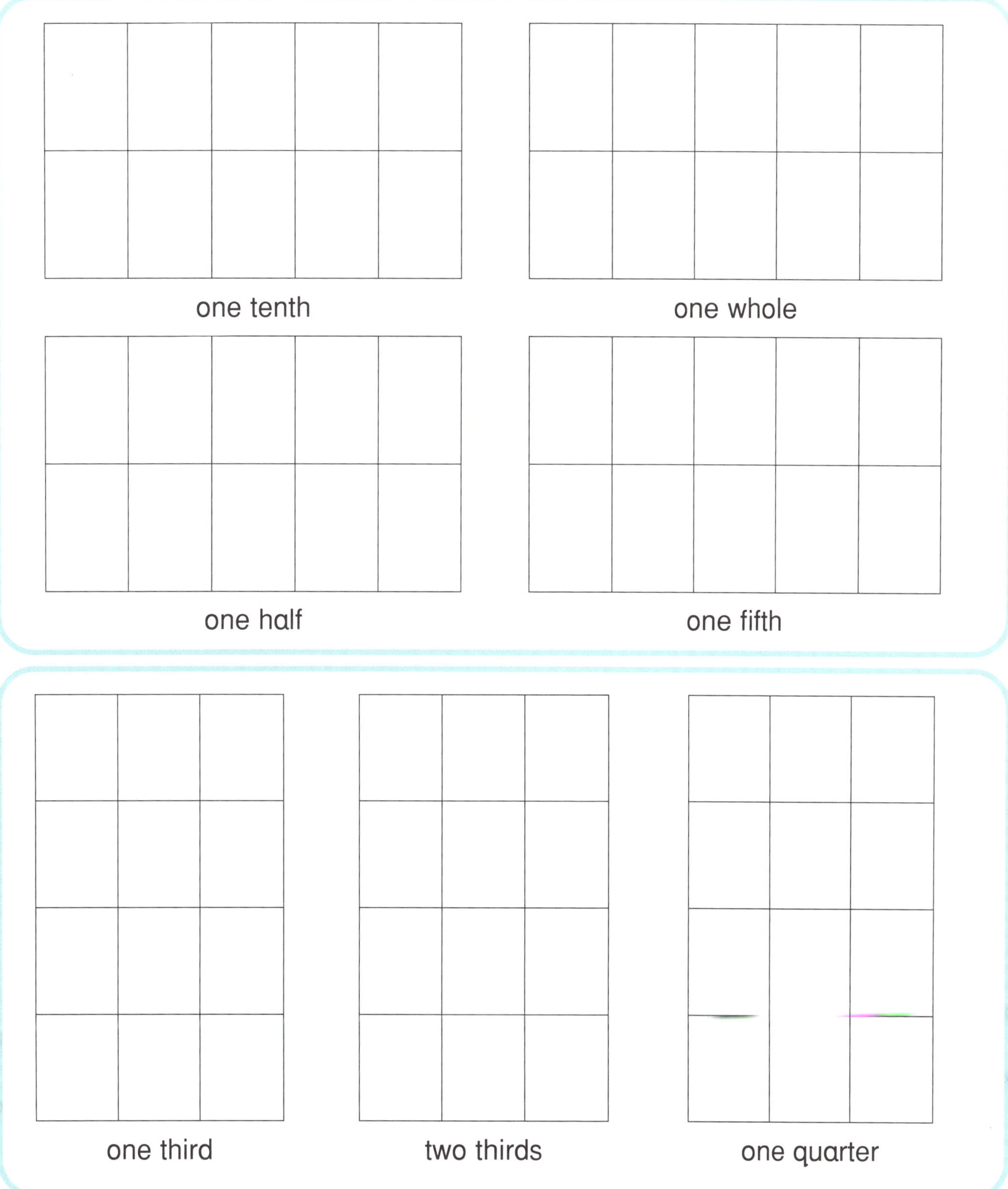

Look at these boxes of chocolates. Some have been eaten.
What fraction of each box of chocolates *hasn't* been eaten?

Example: 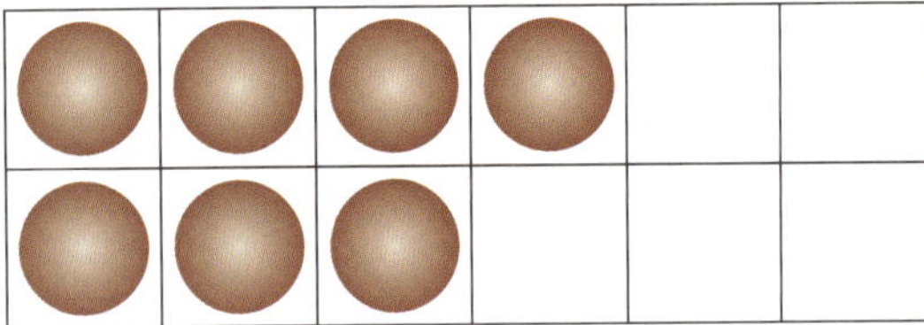 answer: $\frac{5}{8}$ 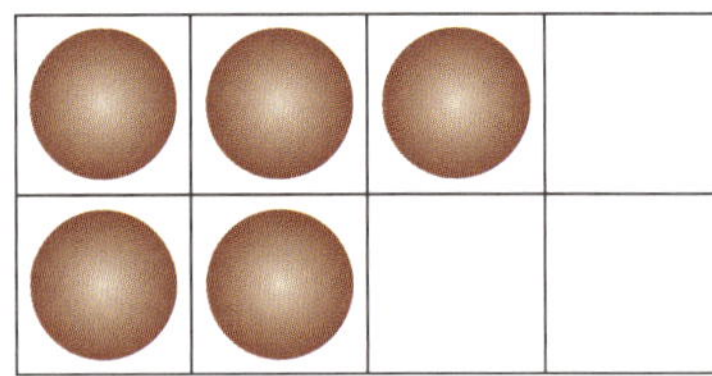

number of chocolates left
number of chocolates when full

A

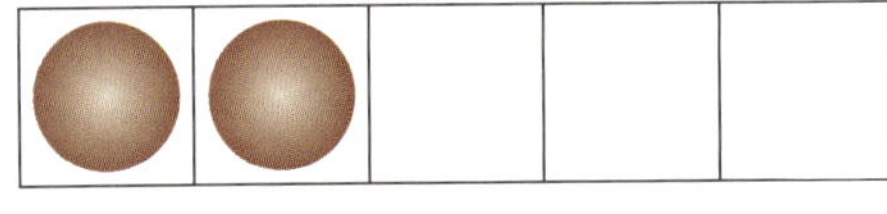

______

B

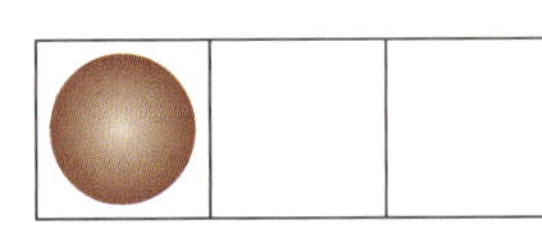

______

C

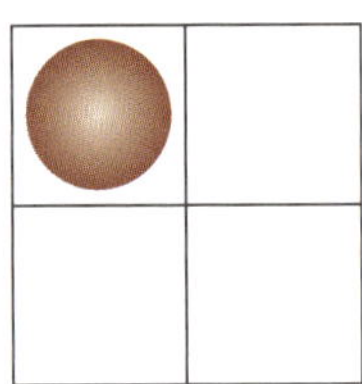

______

D

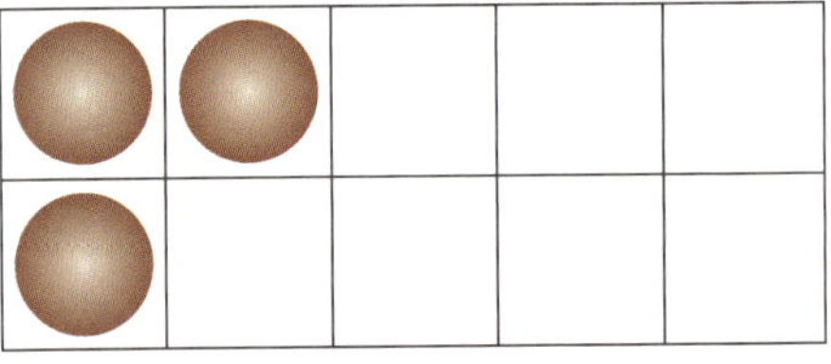

______

E

______

F

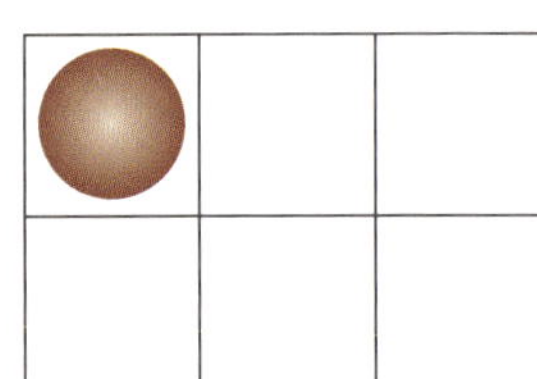

______

G

______

H

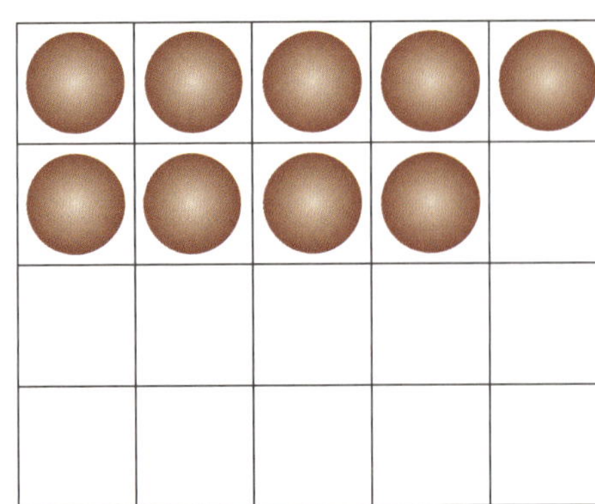

______

Draw the chocolates that are left in the box.
The fraction is written below the box.

Example: 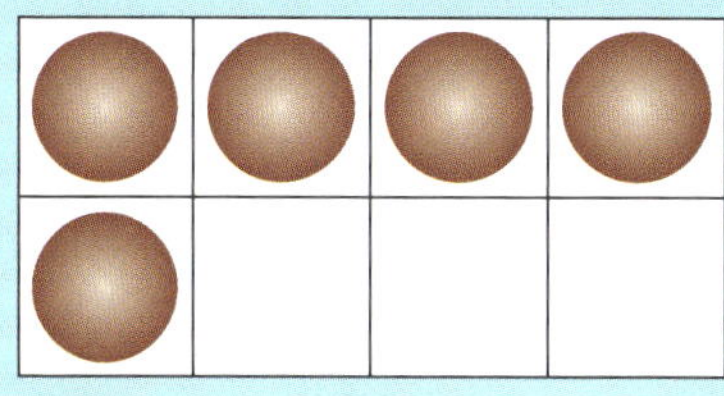

$$\frac{5}{8}$$

A

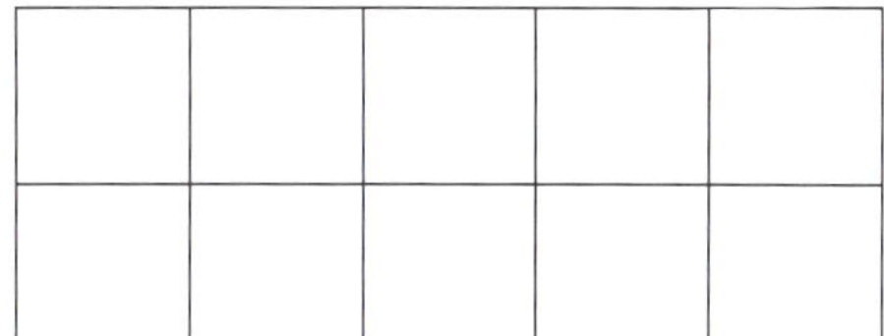

$$\frac{7}{10}$$

B

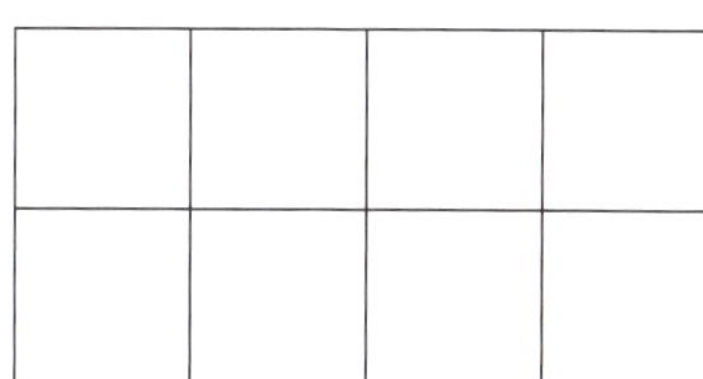

$$\frac{3}{8}$$

C

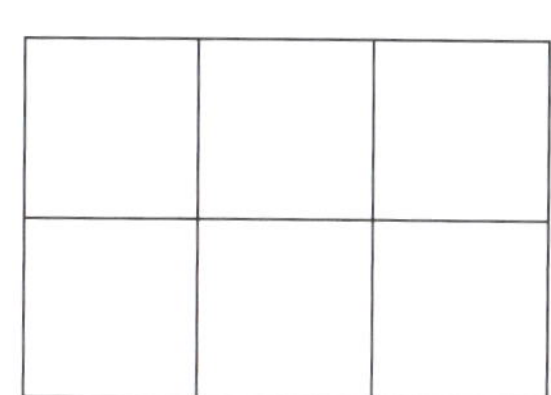

$$\frac{5}{6}$$

D

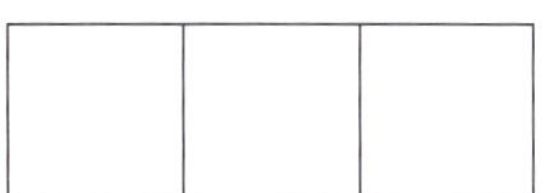

$$\frac{2}{3}$$

E

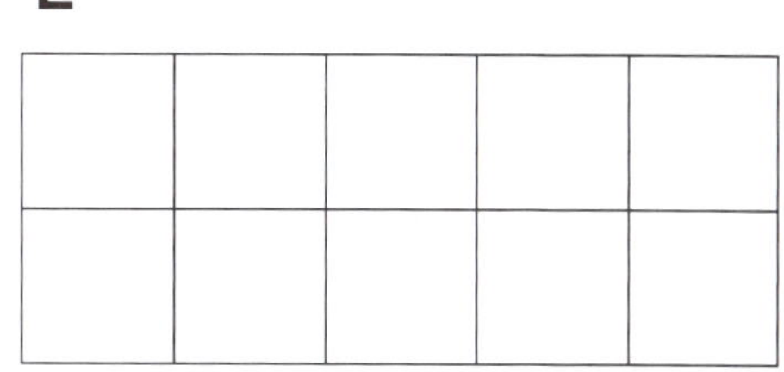

$$\frac{9}{10}$$

F

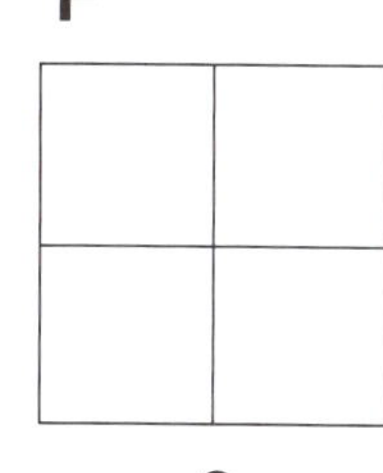

$$\frac{3}{4}$$

G

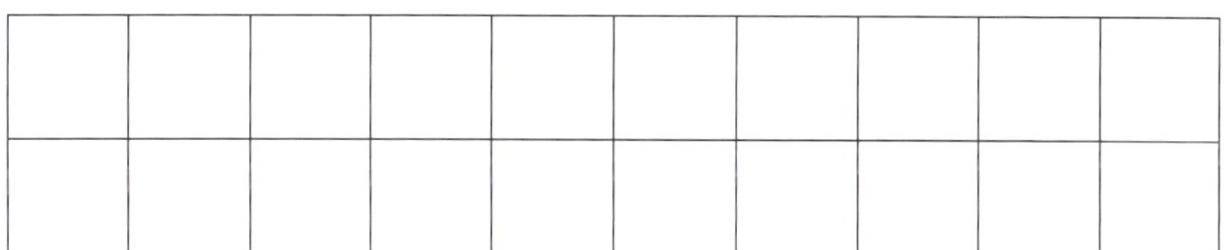

$$\frac{13}{20}$$

H

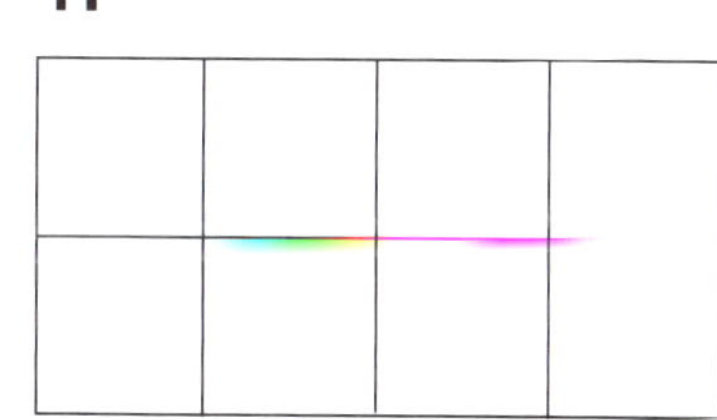

$$\frac{7}{8}$$

Calculate how many buttons should be circled for each amount.
Then complete the number problem.

Circle half the buttons.

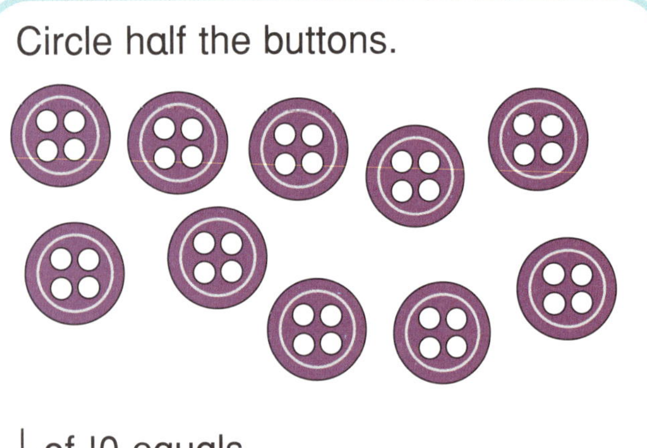

$\frac{1}{2}$ of 10 equals _______________________

Circle a quarter of the buttons.

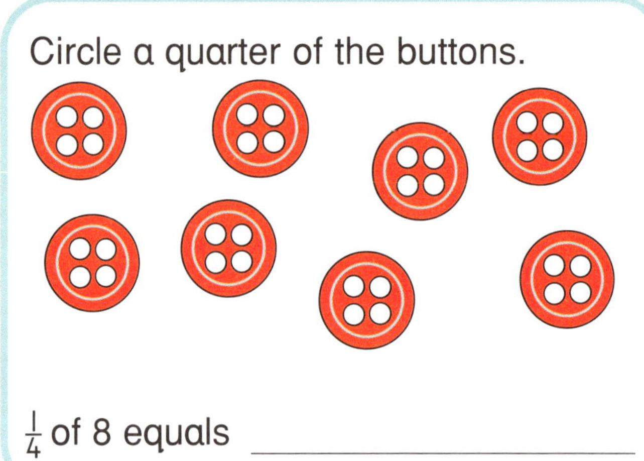

$\frac{1}{4}$ of 8 equals _______________________

Circle a tenth of the buttons.

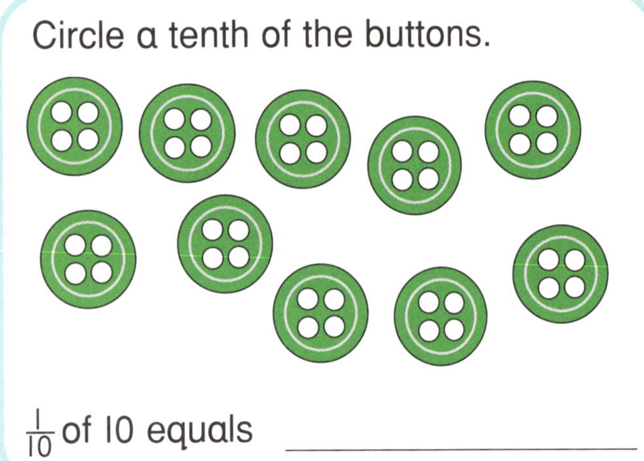

$\frac{1}{10}$ of 10 equals _______________________

Circle a third of the buttons.

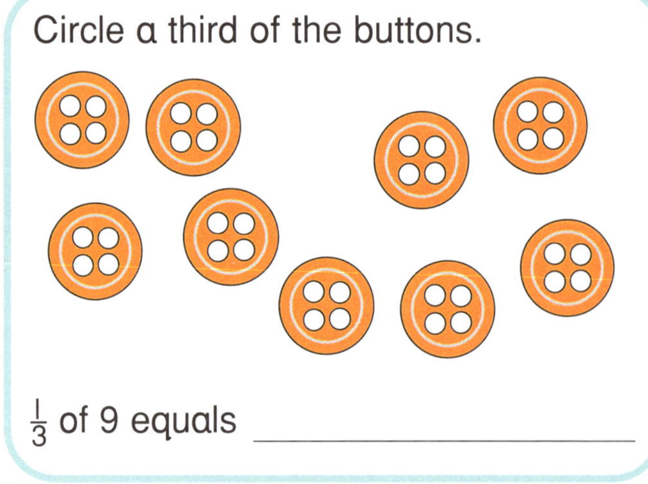

$\frac{1}{3}$ of 9 equals _______________________

Complete these sentences:

To find half of a number you divide by _______________________

To find a third of a number you divide by _______________________

To find a quarter of a number you divide by _______________________

To find a tenth of a number you divide by _______________________

Remember:

$\dfrac{1}{2}$

The top part of a fraction tells us how many pieces we have.

The bottom part of a fraction tells us how many pieces the whole has been divided into.

$\frac{2}{3}$ means the whole number has been cut into 3 pieces and we have 2 of them.

Write how many each circle has been cut into, and how many pieces we have:

$\frac{1}{2}$ The circle has been cut into _________ pieces.

We have _________ of them.

$\frac{1}{3}$ The circle has been cut into _________ pieces.

We have _________ of them.

$\frac{1}{4}$ The circle has been cut into _________ pieces.

We have _________ of them.

$\frac{2}{3}$ The circle has been cut into _________ pieces.

We have _________ of them.

$\frac{3}{4}$ The circle has been cut into _________ pieces.

We have _________ of them.

Making one

Join the fractions which add up to 1.
The first one is done for you.

A

$\dfrac{1}{4}$	$\dfrac{2}{3}$
$\dfrac{1}{6}$	$\dfrac{7}{8}$
$\dfrac{1}{2}$	$\dfrac{4}{5}$
$\dfrac{1}{3}$	$\dfrac{1}{2}$
$\dfrac{1}{5}$	$\dfrac{3}{4}$
$\dfrac{1}{8}$	$\dfrac{5}{6}$

B

$\dfrac{3}{10}$	$\dfrac{3}{5}$
$\dfrac{5}{8}$	$\dfrac{5}{9}$
$\dfrac{2}{5}$	$\dfrac{3}{8}$
$\dfrac{4}{7}$	$\dfrac{7}{10}$
$\dfrac{2}{7}$	$\dfrac{3}{7}$
$\dfrac{4}{9}$	$\dfrac{5}{7}$

C

$\dfrac{3}{10}$	$\dfrac{5}{10}$
$\dfrac{5}{10}$	$\dfrac{2}{10}$
$\dfrac{9}{10}$	$\dfrac{7}{10}$
$\dfrac{8}{10}$	$\dfrac{3}{10}$
$\dfrac{6}{10}$	$\dfrac{1}{10}$
$\dfrac{7}{10}$	$\dfrac{4}{10}$

Making one

My pencils have broken in half! Complete the pencils by matching the pieces which add up to 1.

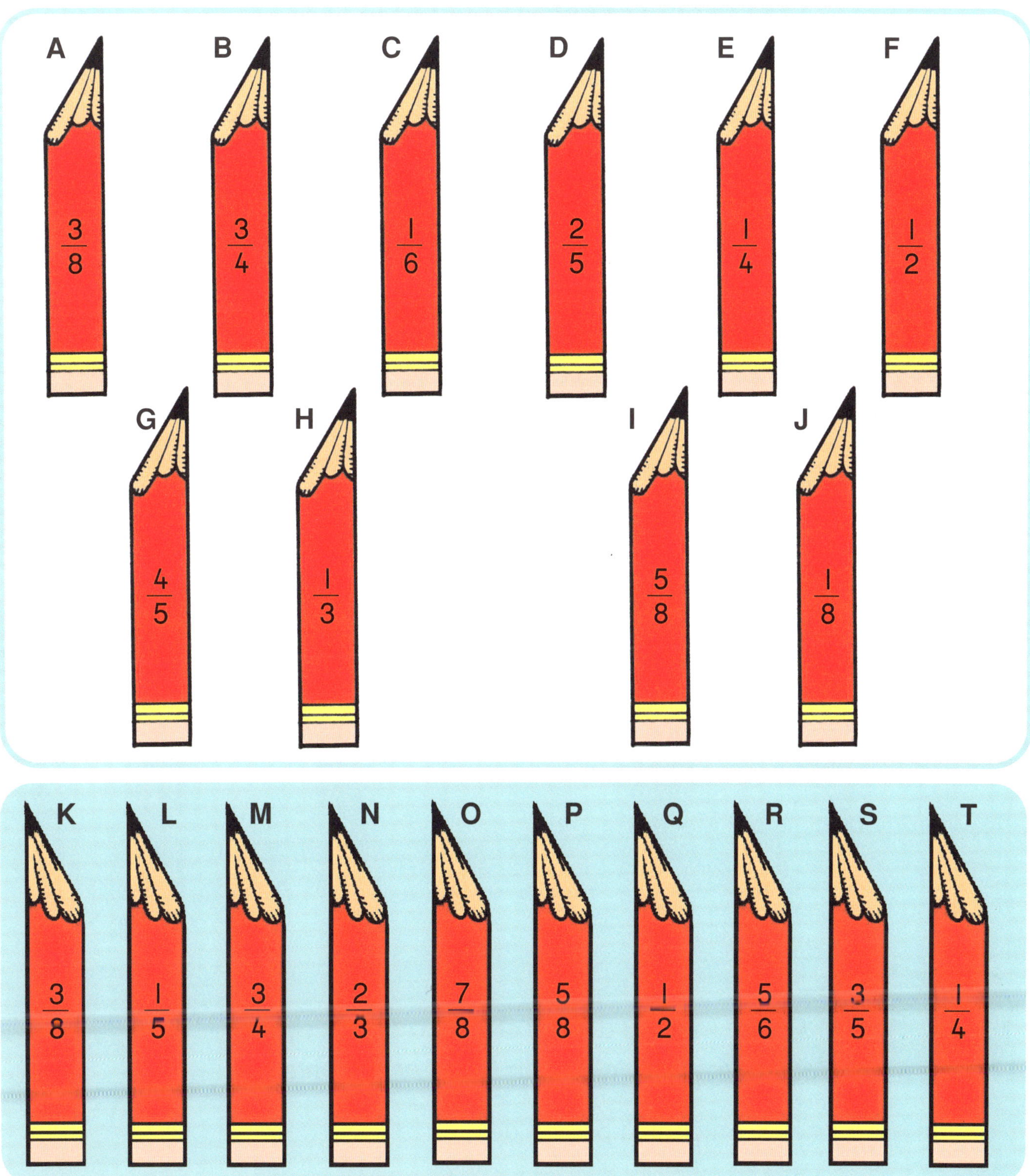

Mel and Nigel earn the following amounts for helping Dad.
They share the money so that they each receive half.
How much money did each child get for each job?

Cleaning the car £6   Each received £_______

Walking the dog £2   Each received £_______

Cleaning the kitchen £8   Each received £_______

Cleaning the windows for a month £18   Each received £_______

After cleaning the windows, Dad brought out 18 biscuits.
Mel ate a third of them and Nigel ate half of them.

How many biscuits did Nigel eat?   _______________________

How many biscuits did Mel eat?   _______________________

How many biscuits were left?   _______________________

Mel and Nigel shared a bag of twenty
chocolates with Razia and Michael.

How many chocolates did each person get? _______________________

Four children divide this bar of chocolate between them.

What fraction of the chocolate did each child get? __________

How many pieces of chocolate did each child get? __________

An identical bar of chocolate is divided between three children.

What fraction of the bar does each child receive? __________

How many pieces of chocolate does each child have? __________

This packet of sweets is shared between 10 children.

What fraction of the sweets did each child receive? __________

How many sweets did each child get? __________________________

How did you work this out? __________________________

____

Look at each group of 3 cakes. For each group decide which shaded piece is the smallest, which is the largest and which comes in between. Write your answers next to the fractions.

A

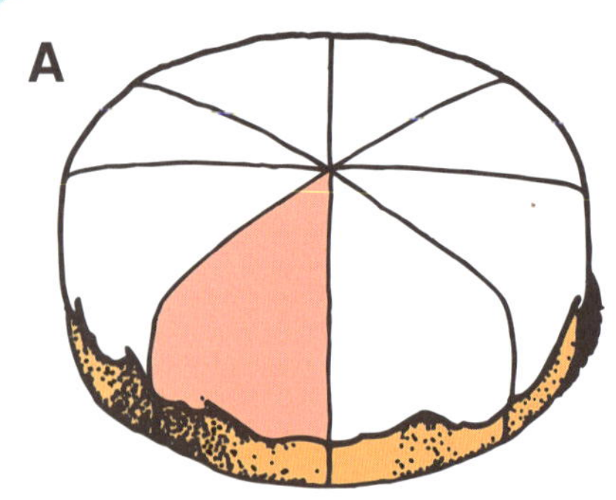 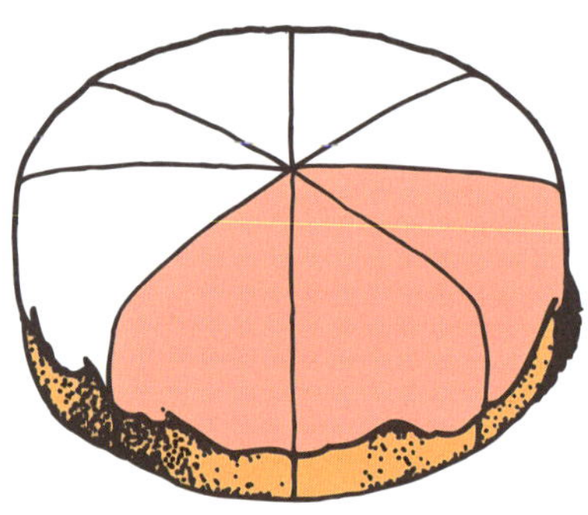 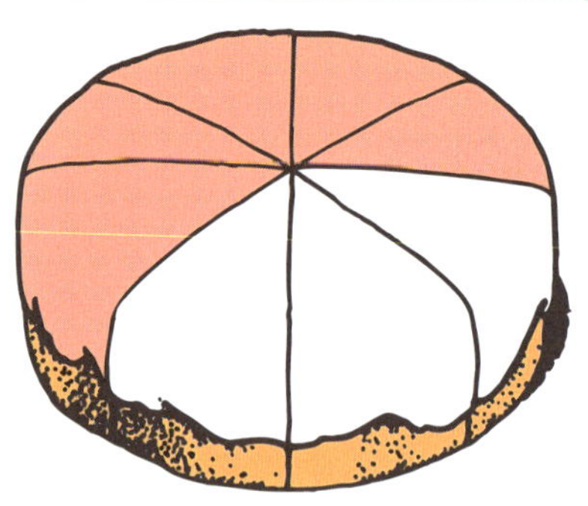

$\dfrac{1}{8}$ ___________ $\dfrac{3}{8}$ ___________ $\dfrac{5}{8}$ ___________

B

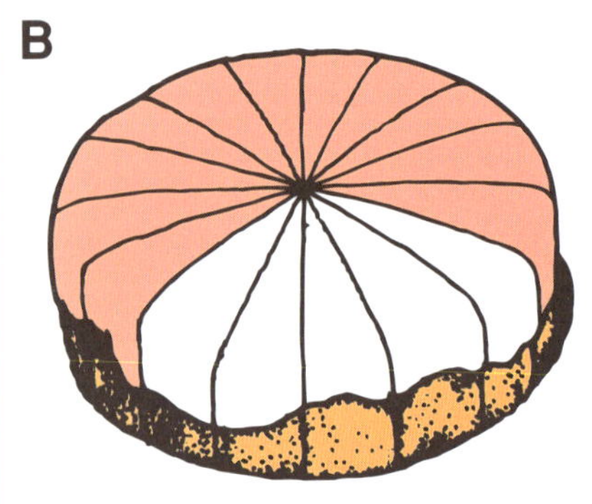 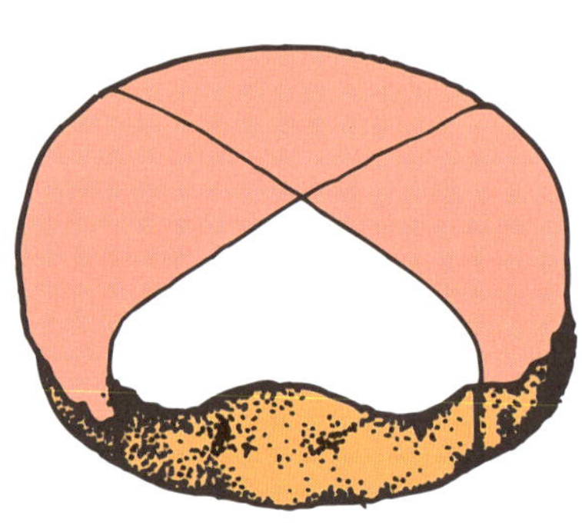 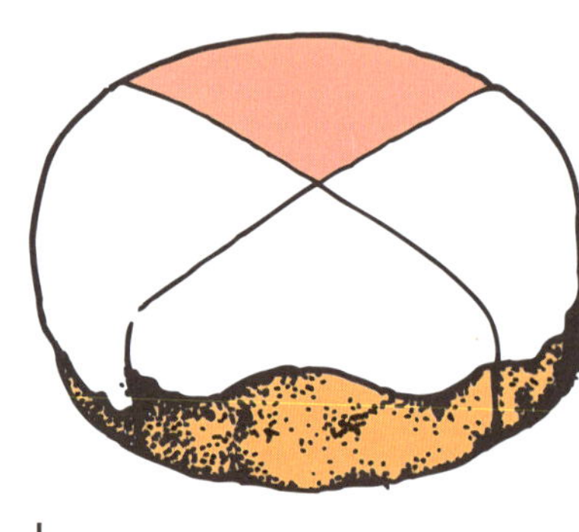

$\dfrac{11}{16}$ ___________ $\dfrac{3}{4}$ ___________ $\dfrac{1}{4}$ ___________

C

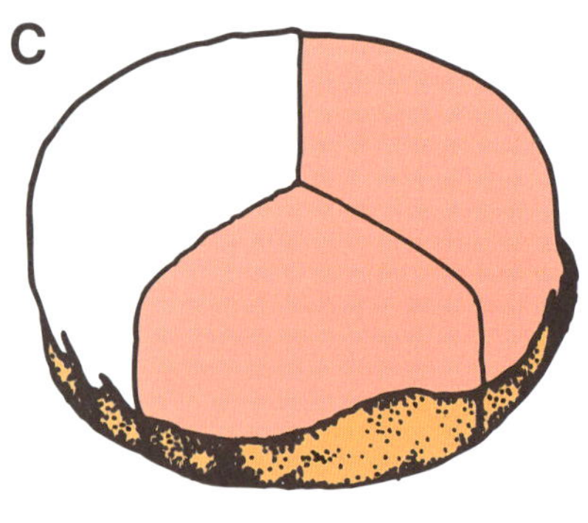 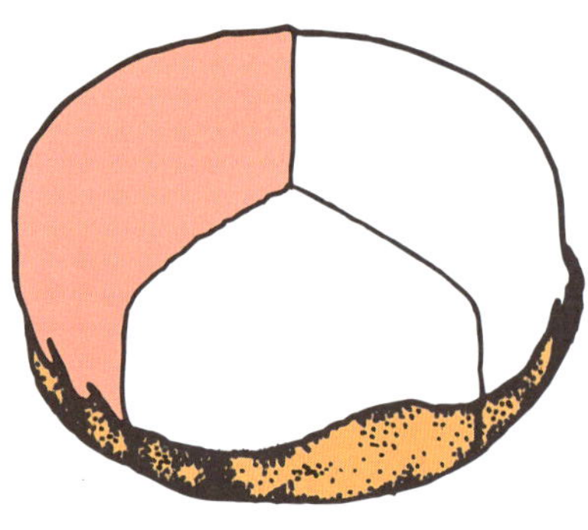 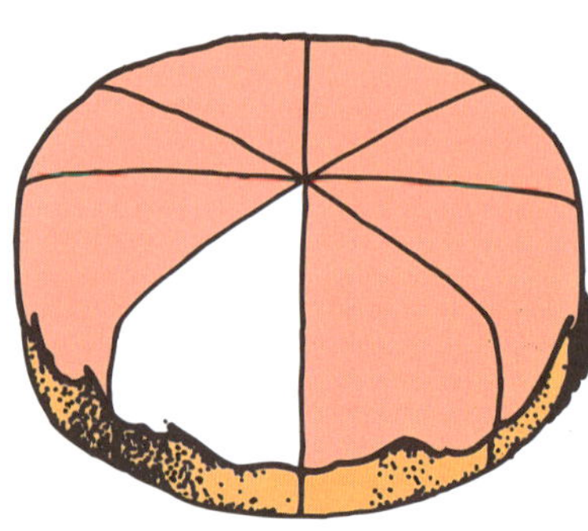

$\dfrac{2}{3}$ ___________ $\dfrac{1}{3}$ ___________ $\dfrac{7}{8}$ ___________

Ordering fractions

If the fraction is bigger than $\frac{1}{2}$ put a tick in the box.
If the fraction is smaller than $\frac{1}{2}$ put a cross in the box.

A $\frac{1}{3}$ ☐ B $\frac{2}{3}$ ☐ C $\frac{5}{8}$ ☐ D $\frac{6}{7}$ ☐

E $\frac{3}{4}$ ☐ F $\frac{1}{4}$ ☐ G $\frac{7}{10}$ ☐ H $\frac{2}{6}$ ☐

I $\frac{3}{10}$ ☐ J $\frac{3}{10}$ ☐ K $\frac{3}{8}$ ☐ L $\frac{8}{12}$ ☐

M $\frac{4}{7}$ ☐ N $\frac{4}{5}$ ☐ O $\frac{5}{12}$ ☐ P $\frac{5}{8}$ ☐

Q $\frac{6}{8}$ ☐ R $\frac{1}{8}$ ☐ S $\frac{2}{9}$ ☐ T $\frac{3}{7}$ ☐

U $\frac{5}{6}$ ☐ V $\frac{3}{5}$ ☐ W $\frac{7}{8}$ ☐ X $\frac{11}{12}$ ☐

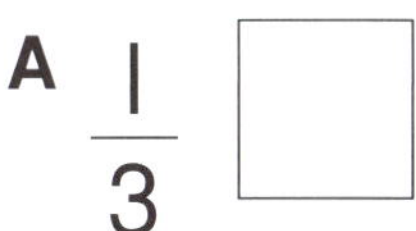

Top tip:
To help you, look at the **numerator** and decide whether it is bigger than half of the **denominator.** If it is, the fraction is bigger than a half.

Fill in the missing numbers and fractions in the sentences below.

This bar of chocolate has been shared

between ___________ children.

They each get ___________ of the chocolate.

This bar of chocolate has been shared

between ___________ children.

They each get ___________ of the chocolate.

This bar of chocolate has been shared

between ___________ children.

They each get ___________ of the chocolate.

This bar of chocolate has been shared

between ___________ children.

They each get ___________ of the chocolate.

Relating fractions to division

Each bar of chocolate must be divided equally between some children.
The fraction of the chocolate that they all must receive is shown on the right.
Draw lines to correctly divide up the chocolate, and say how many pieces
each child gets.

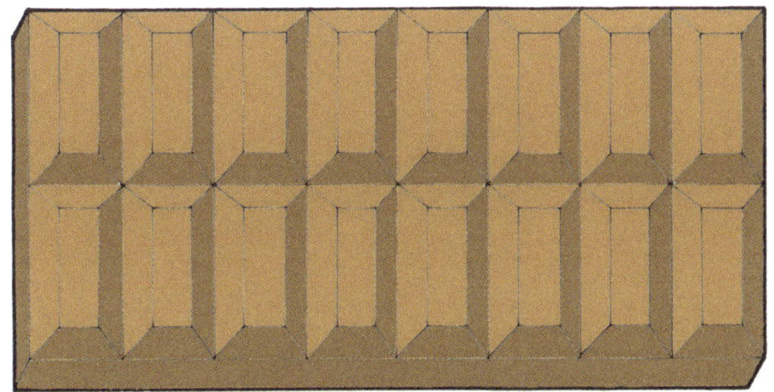

Divide the chocolate so that each child in a group gets $\frac{1}{4}$.

Each child gets ___________ pieces.

Divide this chocolate so that each child in a group gets $\frac{1}{8}$.

Each child gets ___________ pieces.

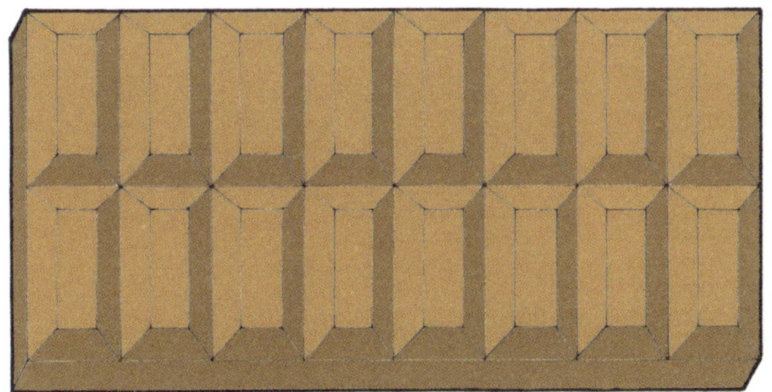

Divide this chocolate so that each child in a group gets $\frac{1}{2}$.

Each child gets ___________ pieces.

Divide this chocolate so that each child in a group gets $\frac{1}{16}$.

Each child gets ___________ pieces.

In every, for every

Complete the sentences below each pattern
by filling in the missing numbers.

1 in every 3 is coloured.

So _______________ in every 6 are coloured,

and _______________ in every 9 are coloured.

2 in every 3 are coloured.

So _______________ in every 6 are coloured,

and _______________ in every 9 are coloured.

5 in every 6 are coloured.

So _______________ in every 12 are coloured,

and _______________ in every 18 are coloured.

Complete the posters below by filling in the missing numbers.

A

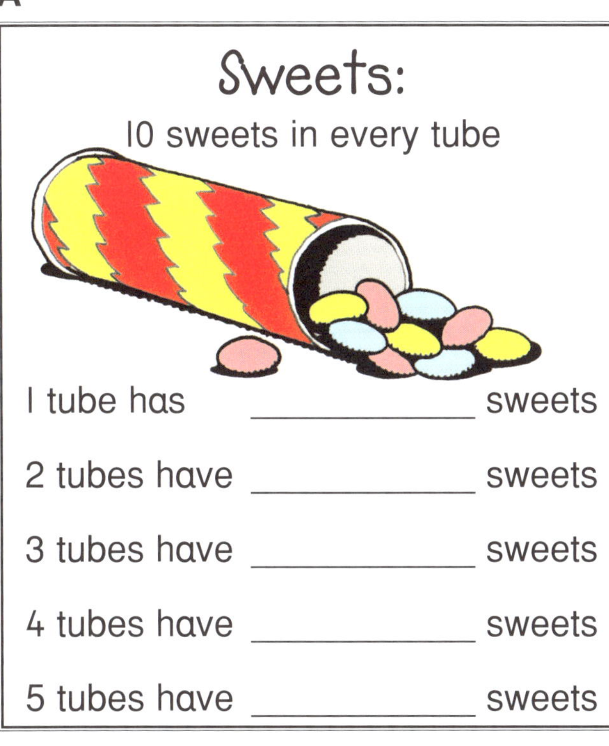

B

C

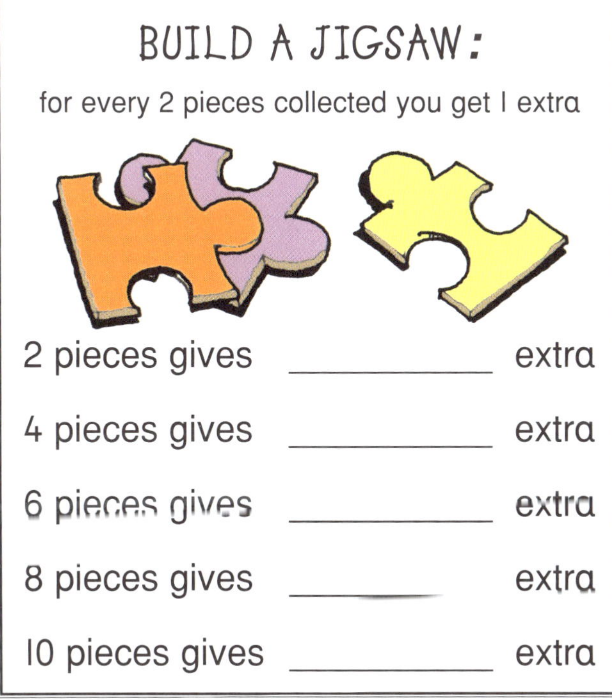

D

What fraction of the larger shape is the smaller shape?

The first one has been done for you

A

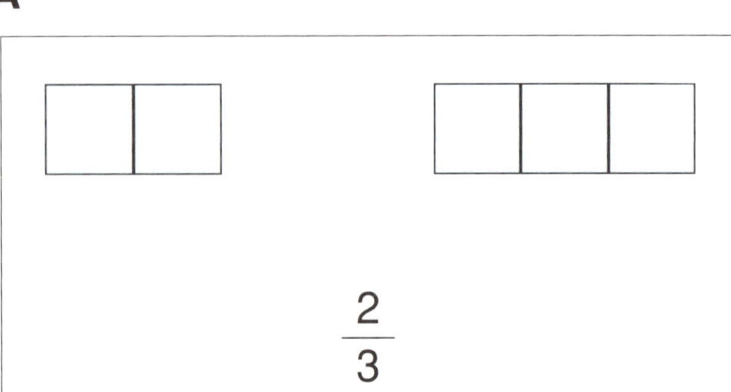

$$\frac{2}{3}$$

B

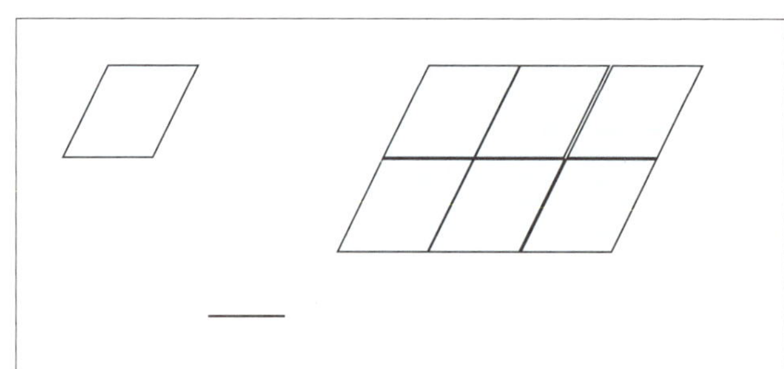

C

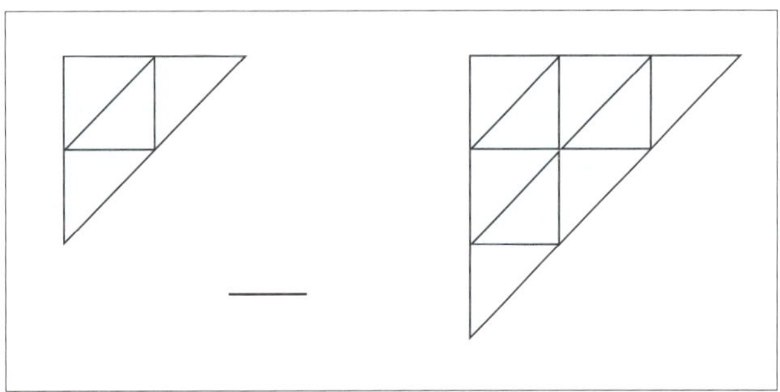

D

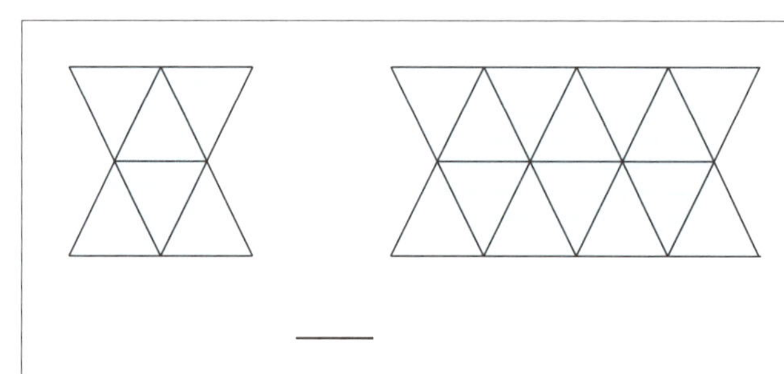

E

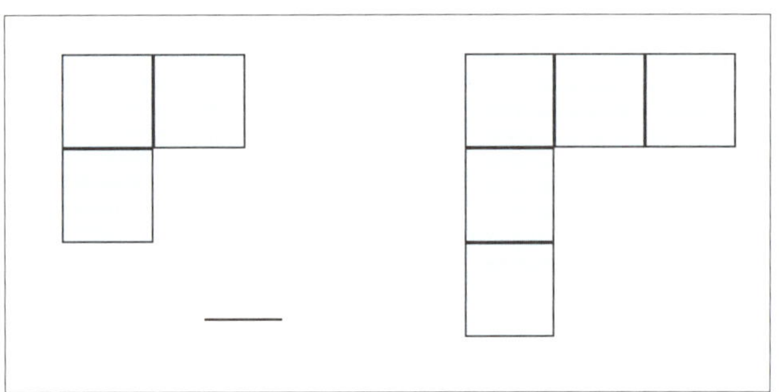

F

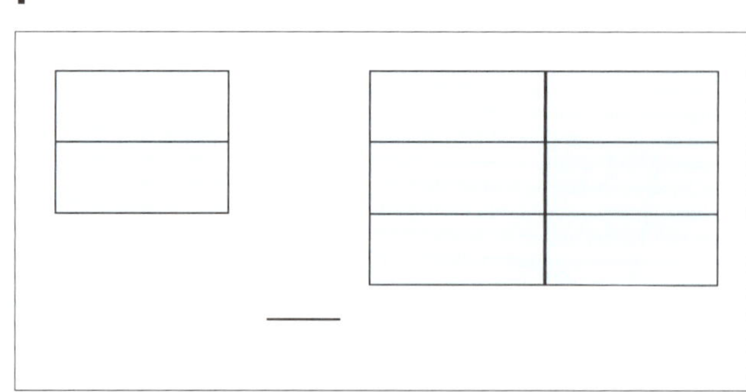

G

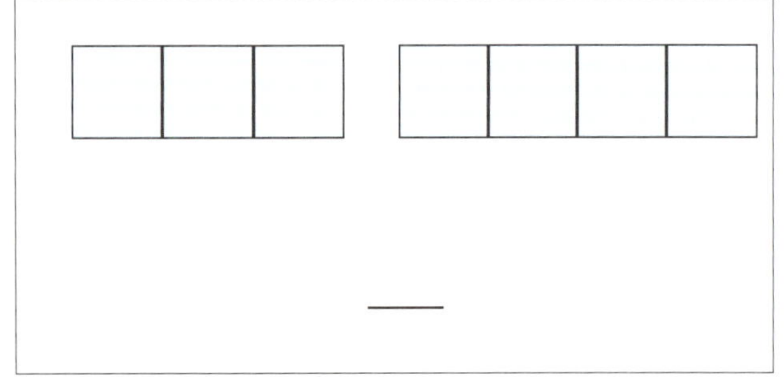

H

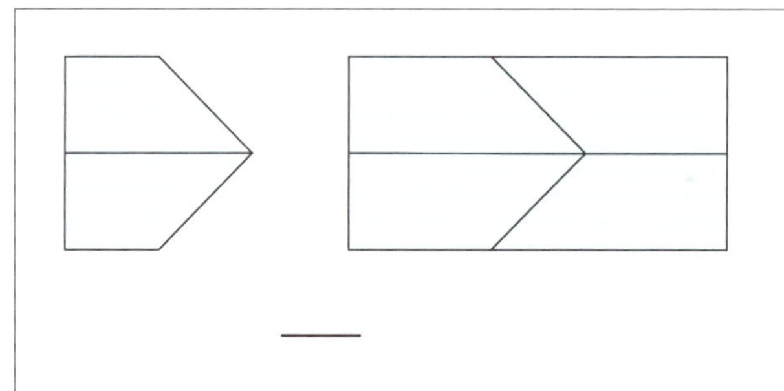

Fractions of shapes

Add up the value of each group of coins in the box.
Then use this to find what fraction the smaller amount is
of the larger amount. The first one has been done for you.

A

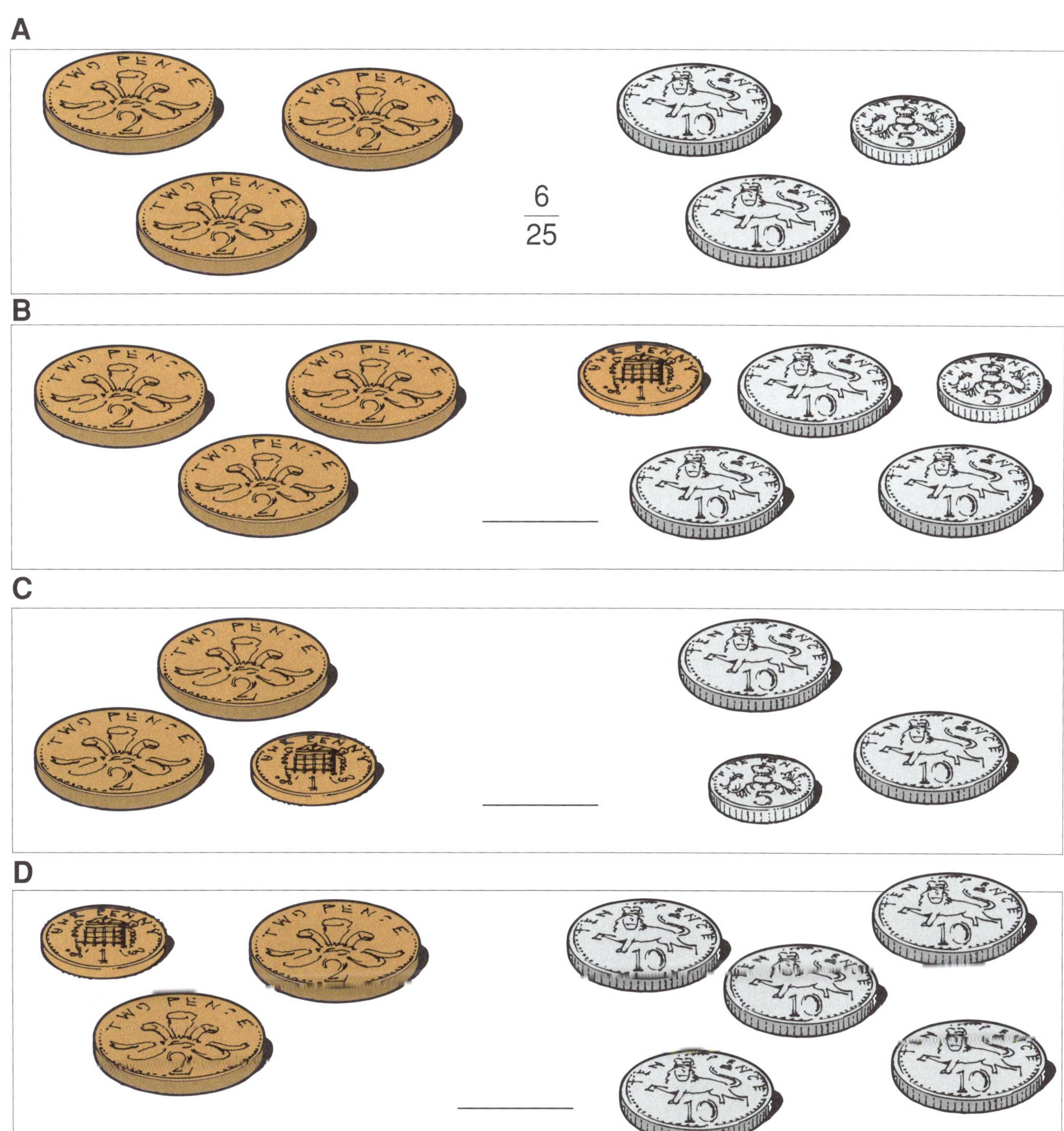

$$\frac{6}{25}$$

B

C

D

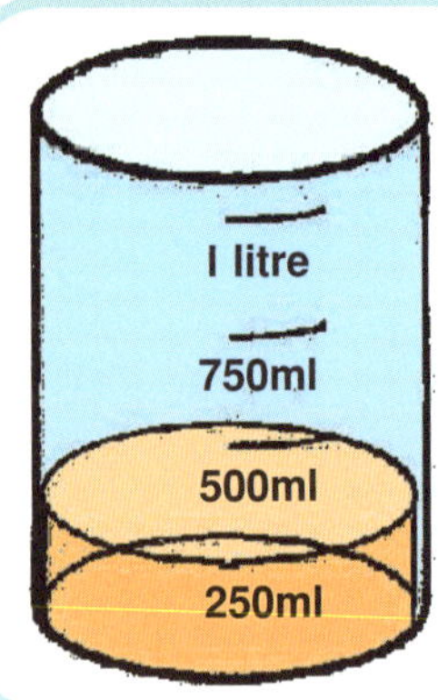

How much of this jar is full? _____________ml

What fraction of a litre is this? _____________

Look at these jars. What fraction of each jar is filled with liquid?

How many millilitres of liquid are there in each jar?

Each mark on the sides of the jars shows 100ml.

A   **B**   **C**

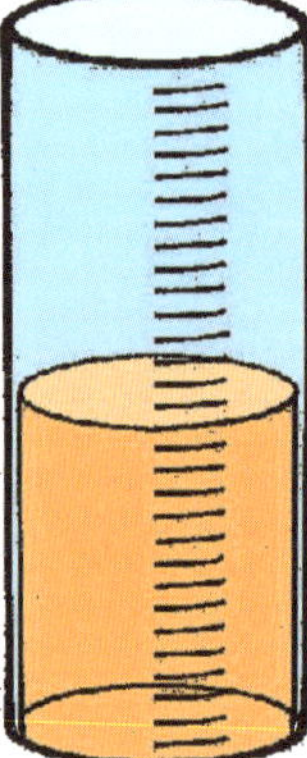

_____________   _____________   _____________

_____________   _____________   _____________

At a party there are 30 children. Each child has a cup that holds $\frac{1}{10}$ litre of juice.

How many litres of juice do you need to fill all the cups? _____________

There are four litres of custard.
How many $\frac{1}{4}$-litre bowls can be filled? _____________

About what fraction of the children will get custard? _____________

Remember: I metre = 100 centimetres
         I kilometre = 1000 metres

Fill in each box with the correct answer.

A A car travels $\frac{1}{2}$ km. How many metres has it travelled so far?

B It travels another 750 metres. How many metres has it travelled so far?

C It travels another $\frac{3}{4}$ km. How many metres has it travelled now?

25cm is what fraction of I metre? _______________________________

What is half I metre in centimetres? _______________________________

Order the amounts of money from the smallest to the largest.
Label them I (smallest) to 5 (largest).

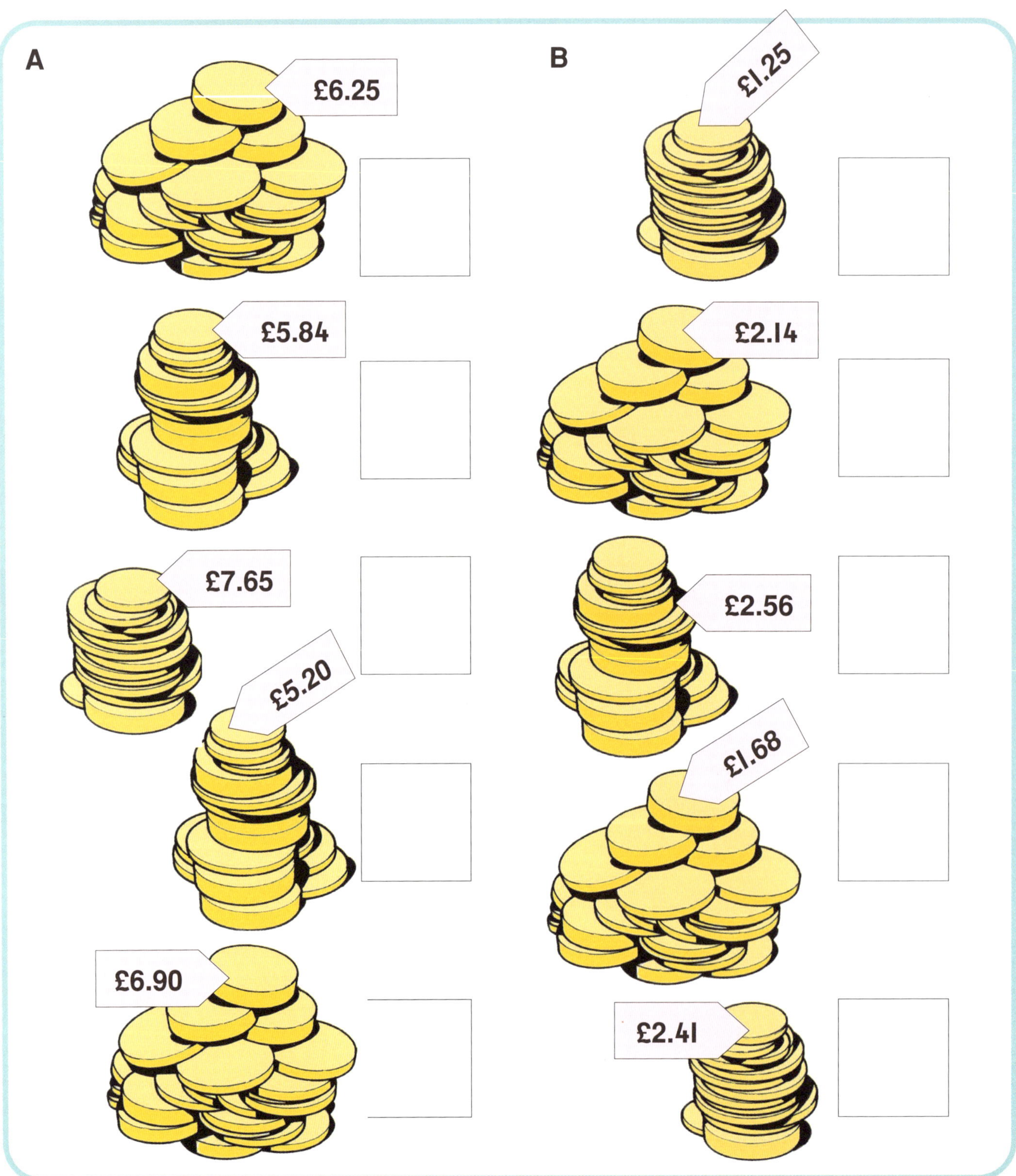

Ordering money

Who has saved the most money in their piggy bank?
Write the children's names in order, from the largest
amount saved to the least amount saved.

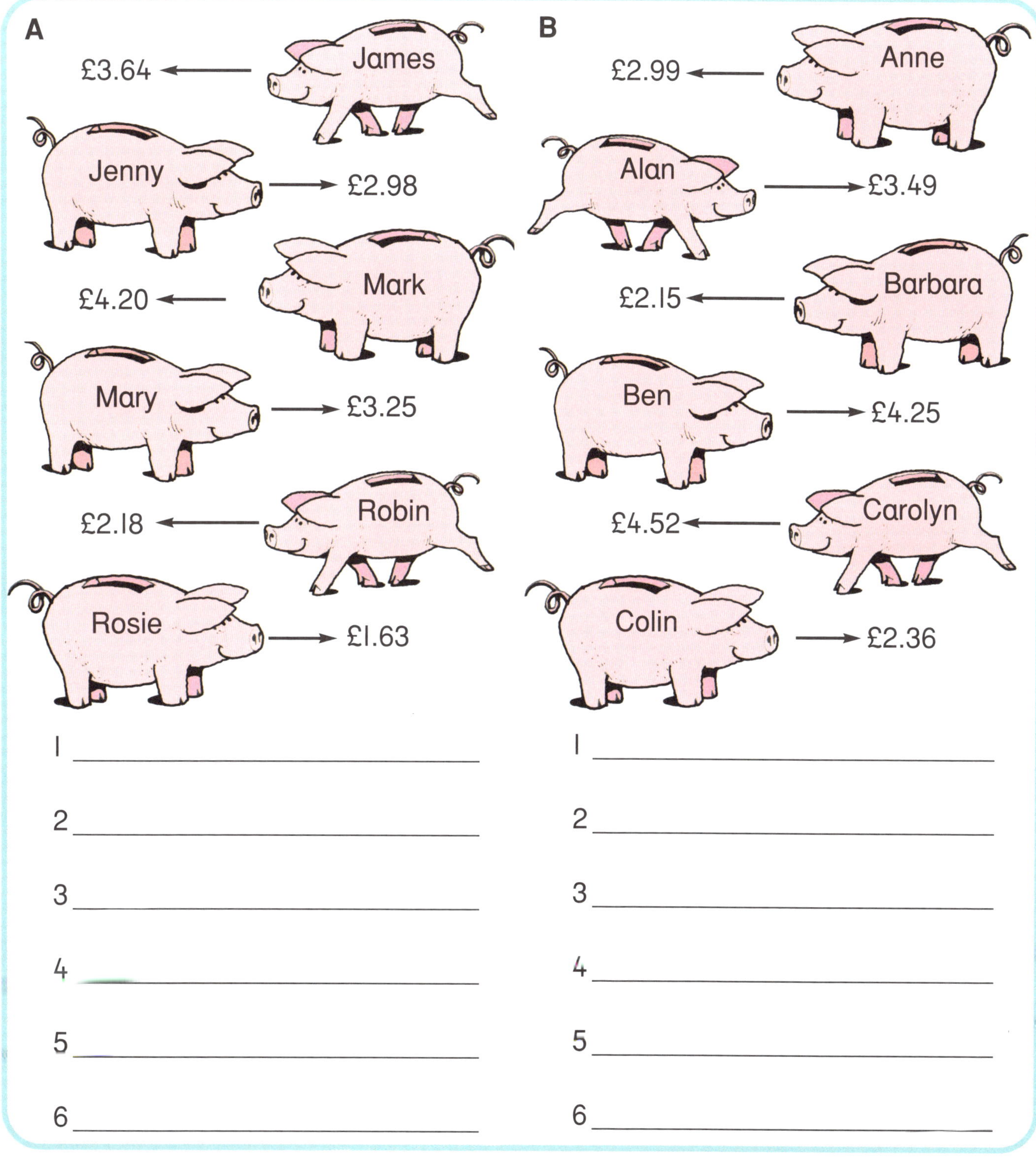

A	B
1 ___________	1 ___________
2 ___________	2 ___________
3 ___________	3 ___________
4 ___________	4 ___________
5 ___________	5 ___________
6 ___________	6 ___________

How much of each pizza has been eaten?
Write the answer as a fraction and as a decimal.

Top Tip:
$\frac{1}{4}$ = 0.25
$\frac{1}{2}$ = 0.5
$\frac{3}{4}$ = 0.75
I whole = I

A

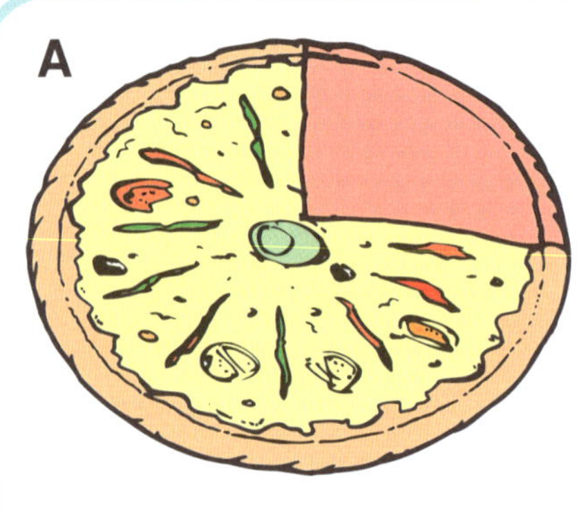

$\frac{1}{4}$ / 0.25

B

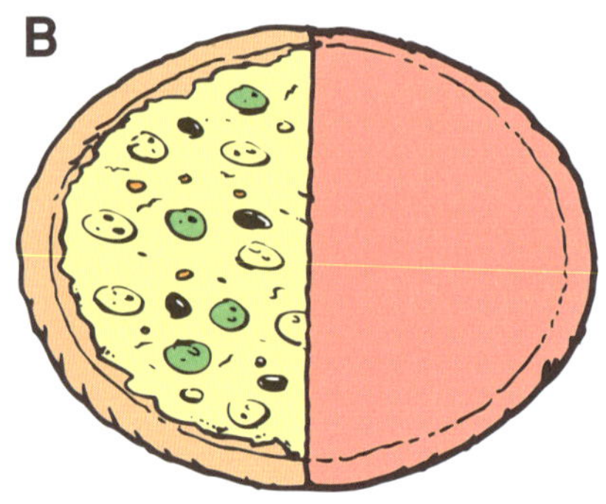

_______ / _______

C

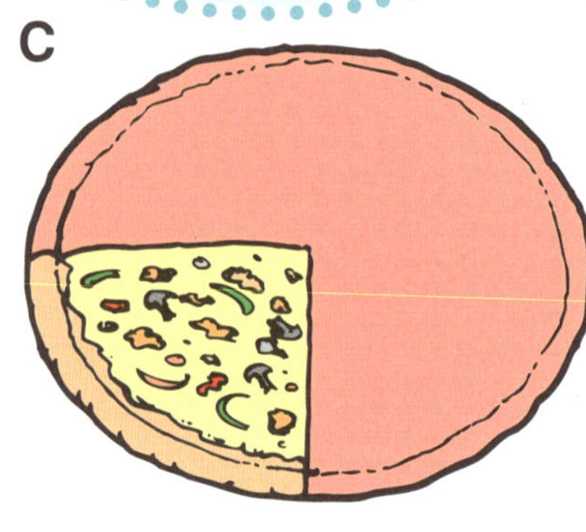

_______ / _______

D

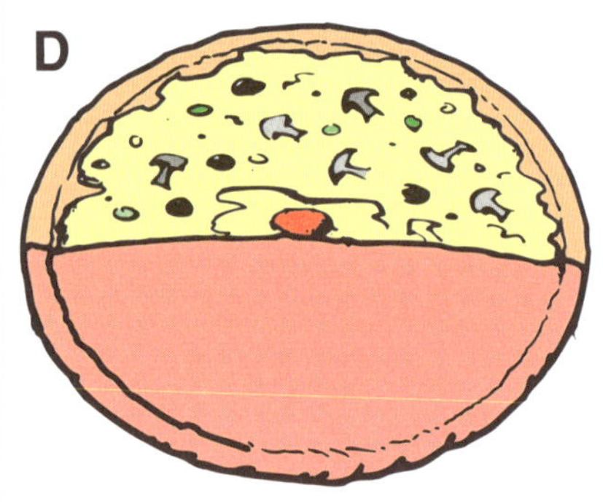

_______ / _______

E

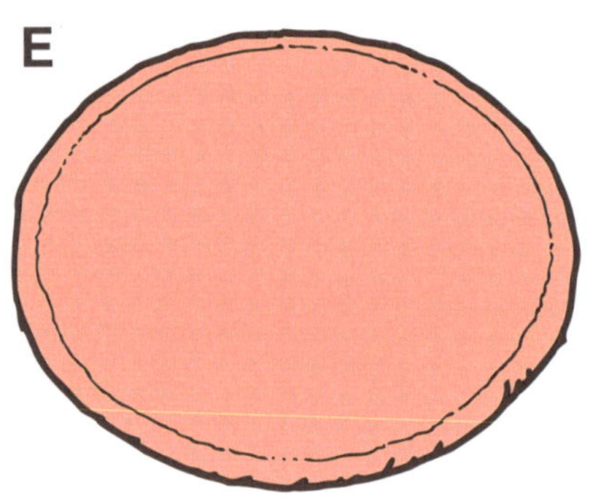

_______ / _______

F

_______ / _______

G

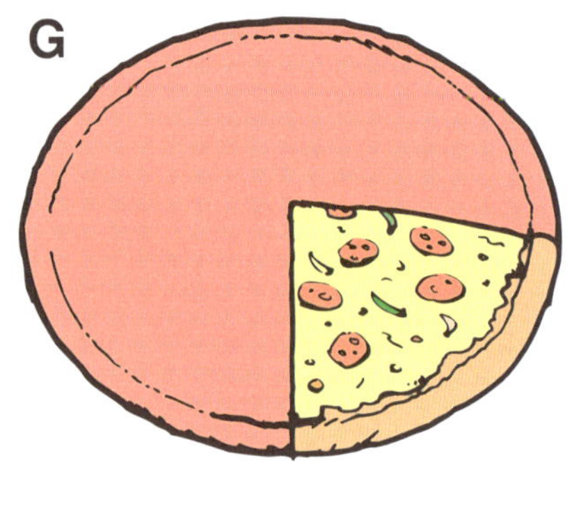

_______ / _______

H

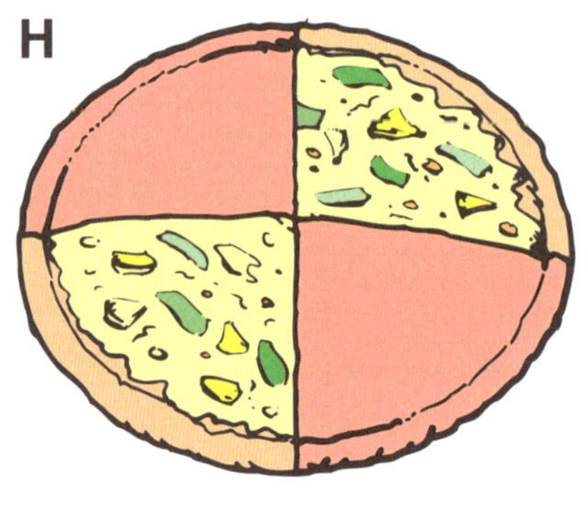

_______ / _______

I

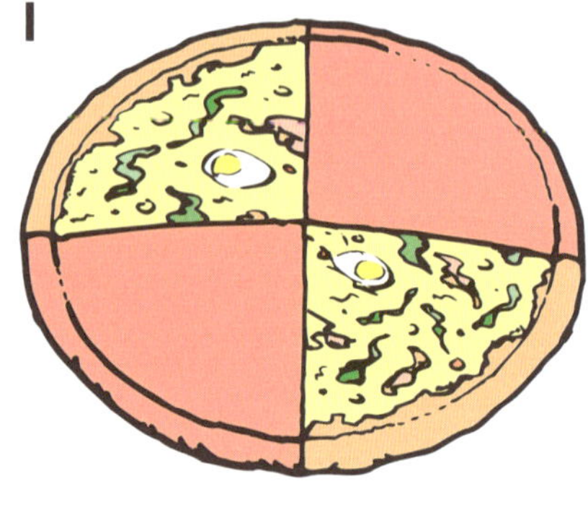

_______ / _______

Below each diagram write in the decimal and the fraction of the shaded area.

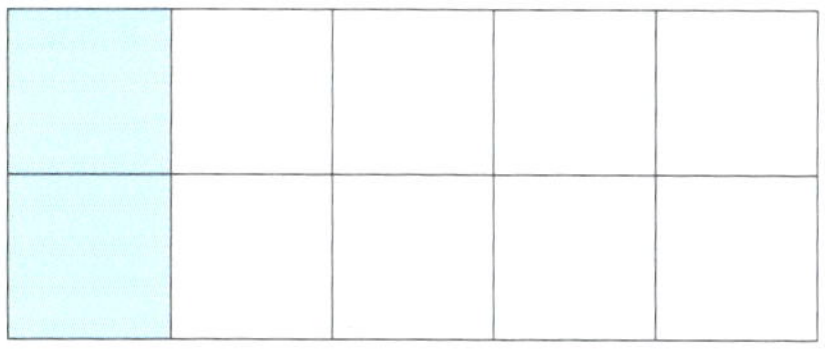

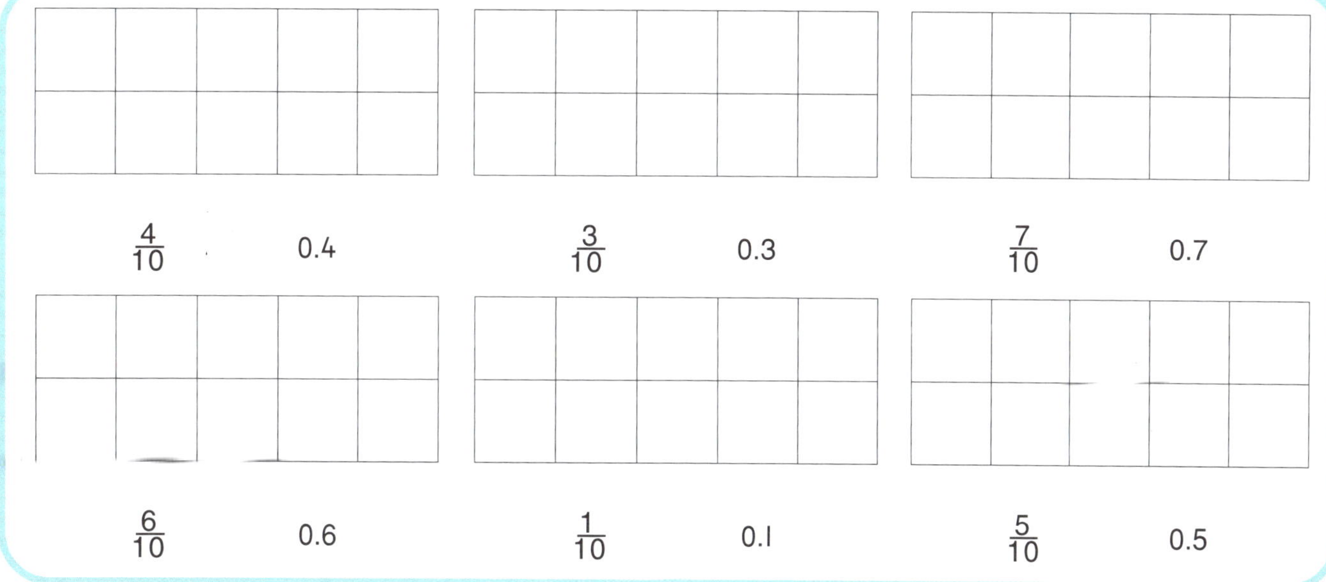

$\frac{2}{10}$ 0.2

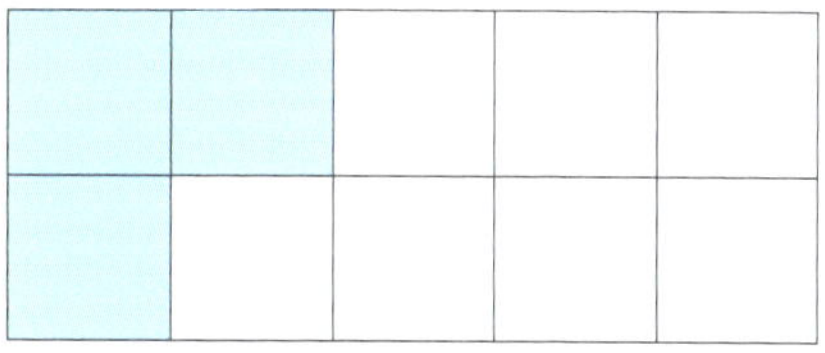

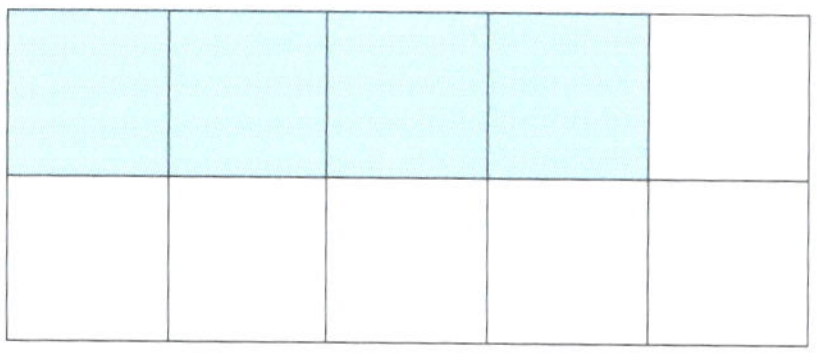

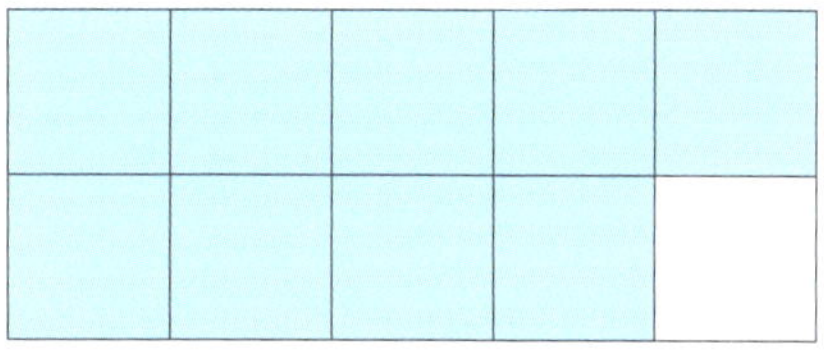

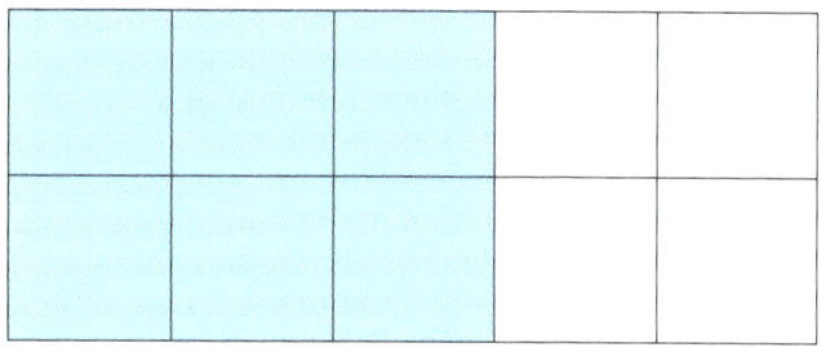

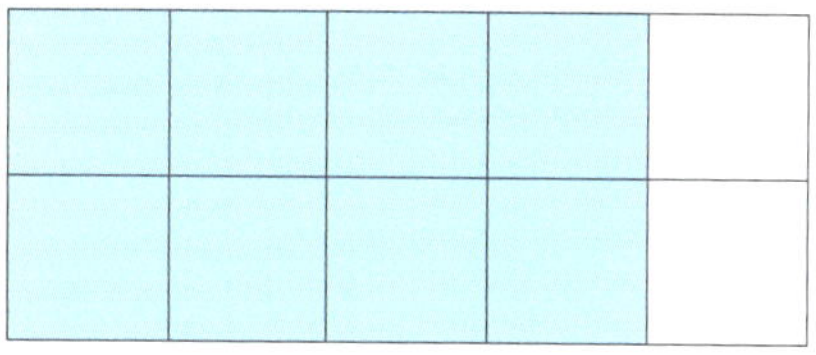

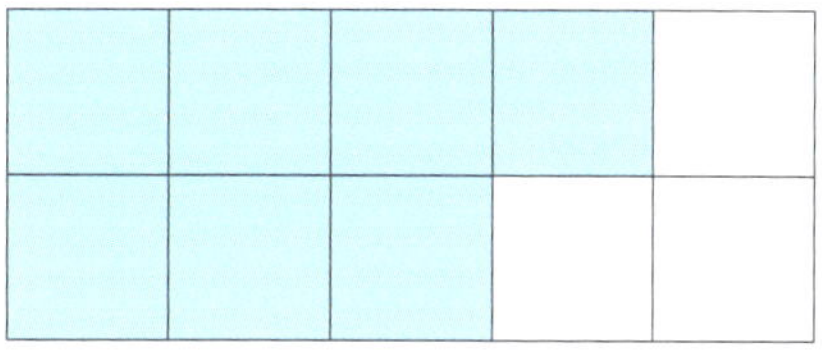

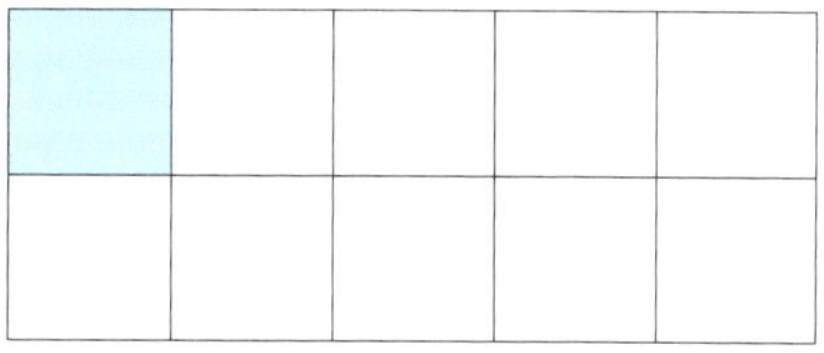

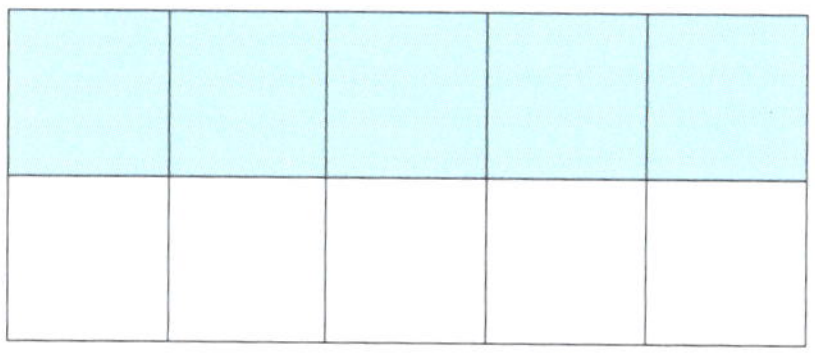

_______   _______

_______   _______

_______   _______   _______   _______

_______   _______   _______   _______

_______   _______   _______   _______

Colour in the correct fraction of the diagrams below.

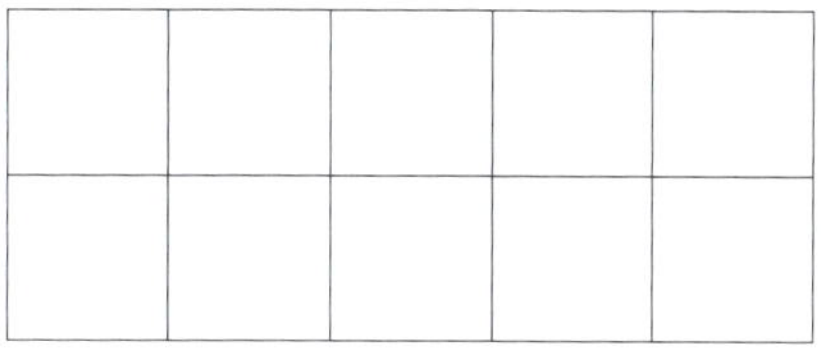

$\frac{4}{10}$ 0.4 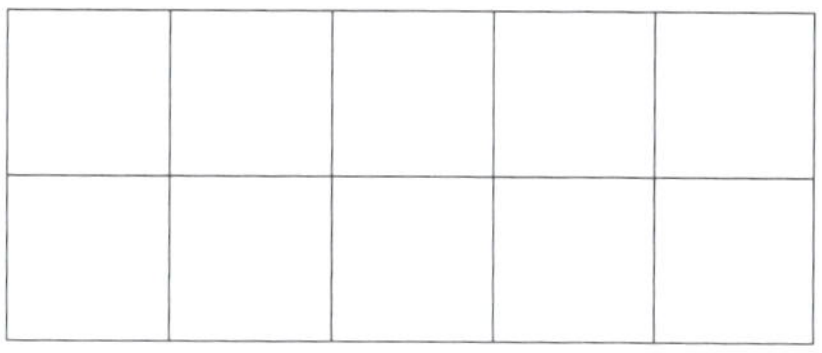 $\frac{3}{10}$ 0.3 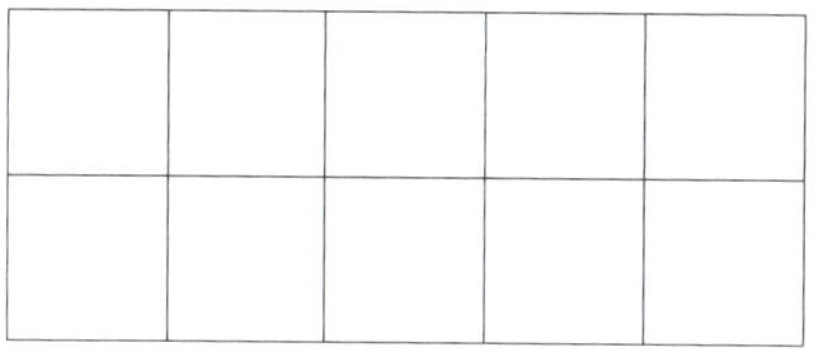 $\frac{7}{10}$ 0.7

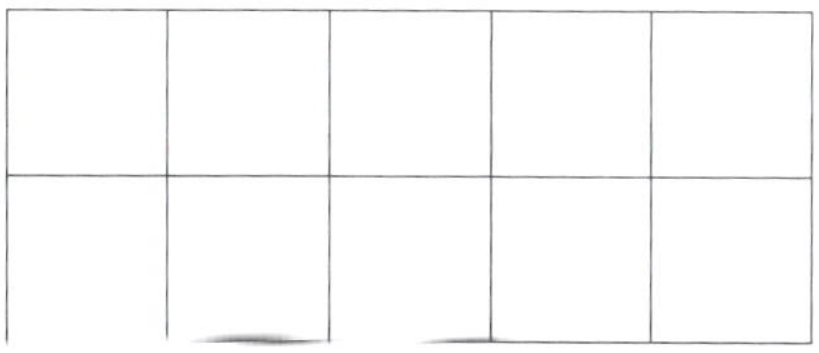

$\frac{6}{10}$ 0.6 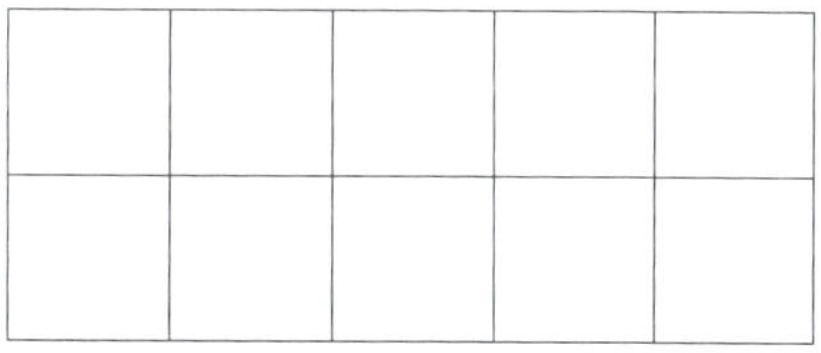 $\frac{1}{10}$ 0.1 $\frac{5}{10}$ 0.5

Show your workings here:

Michael left his maths book out and his dog walked all over it with muddy paws! Can you help Michael work out what numbers or signs have been hidden by the muddy pawmarks?

6 + 🐾 = 13 _____   12 + 🐾 = 18 _____

20 + 🐾 = 35 _____   35 + 🐾 = 60 _____

🐾 + 8 = 12 _____   🐾 + 15 = 20 _____

🐾 + 20 = 30 _____   🐾 + 45 = 100 _____

10 − 🐾 = 7 _____   16 − 🐾 = 9 _____

30 − 🐾 = 24 _____   60 − 🐾 = 35 _____

🐾 − 3 = 5 _____   🐾 − 8 = 12 _____

🐾 − 30 = 50 _____   🐾 − 25 = 75 _____

6 🐾 5 = 11 _____   14 🐾 8 = 22 _____

16 🐾 9 = 25 _____   35 🐾 15 = 50 _____

6 🐾 5 = 1 _____   14 🐾 8 = 6 _____

16 🐾 9 = 7 _____   35 🐾 15 = 20 _____

Answer these riddles. The answers are either one number
or a pair of numbers.

When you add us together we make 12.
The difference between us is 6.   _______ _______

When you add us together we make 8.
When you multiply us together we make 15.   _______ _______

I am bigger than 46 and smaller than 48.   _______

I am twice as big as 12.   _______

When you add me to myself I make 16.   _______

When you add us together we make 24.
One of us is twice as big as the other.   _______ _______

The difference between us is 5.
When you multiply us together we make 14.   _______ _______

One of us is twice as big as the other.
The difference between us is 7.   _______ _______

When you add me to any number, I do not change it.   _______

When you multiply me by myself I make 25.   _______

Show your workings here:

In a magic square the numbers in each row, each column and each diagonal add up to the same answer.

<table>
<tr><td>8</td><td>1</td><td>6</td></tr>
<tr><td>3</td><td>5</td><td>7</td></tr>
<tr><td>4</td><td>9</td><td>2</td></tr>
</table>

This is a magic square because the rows add up to 15:

$8 + 1 + 6 = 15$ $3 + 5 + 7 = 15$ $4 + 9 + 2 = 15$

the up and down columns add up to 15:

$8 + 3 + 4 = 15$ $1 + 5 + 9 = 15$ $6 + 7 + 2 = 15$

and so do the diagonals across the square:

$8 + 5 + 2 = 15$ $4 + 5 + 6 = 15$

Look at these squares. Put a tick by the ones which are magic and a cross by the ones which are not.

1

<table>
<tr><td>12</td><td>5</td><td>10</td></tr>
<tr><td>7</td><td>9</td><td>11</td></tr>
<tr><td>8</td><td>13</td><td>6</td></tr>
</table>

_____

2

<table>
<tr><td>3</td><td>5</td><td>9</td></tr>
<tr><td>4</td><td>8</td><td>2</td></tr>
<tr><td>7</td><td>1</td><td>6</td></tr>
</table>

_____

3

<table>
<tr><td>17</td><td>3</td><td>13</td></tr>
<tr><td>7</td><td>11</td><td>15</td></tr>
<tr><td>6</td><td>9</td><td>25</td></tr>
</table>

_____

4

<table>
<tr><td>7</td><td>12</td><td>5</td></tr>
<tr><td>8</td><td>9</td><td>7</td></tr>
<tr><td>10</td><td>3</td><td>11</td></tr>
</table>

_____

5

<table>
<tr><td>29</td><td>8</td><td>23</td></tr>
<tr><td>14</td><td>20</td><td>26</td></tr>
<tr><td>17</td><td>32</td><td>11</td></tr>
</table>

_____

6

<table>
<tr><td>13</td><td>15</td><td>12</td></tr>
<tr><td>21</td><td>11</td><td>3</td></tr>
<tr><td>6</td><td>9</td><td>25</td></tr>
</table>

_____

Can you work out the missing numbers in these magic squares?

<table>
<tr><td>16</td><td>2</td><td>12</td></tr>
<tr><td>6</td><td>10</td><td></td></tr>
<tr><td>8</td><td></td><td></td></tr>
</table>

<table>
<tr><td>12</td><td>5</td><td></td></tr>
<tr><td>7</td><td>9</td><td></td></tr>
<tr><td>8</td><td></td><td></td></tr>
</table>

<table>
<tr><td></td><td>7</td><td>17</td></tr>
<tr><td></td><td>15</td><td></td></tr>
<tr><td>13</td><td>23</td><td></td></tr>
</table>

<table>
<tr><td>26</td><td>12</td><td>22</td></tr>
<tr><td>16</td><td>20</td><td></td></tr>
<tr><td></td><td></td><td></td></tr>
</table>

<table>
<tr><td>10</td><td></td><td>6</td></tr>
<tr><td></td><td>12</td><td></td></tr>
<tr><td>18</td><td></td><td>14</td></tr>
</table>

<table>
<tr><td>3</td><td></td><td></td></tr>
<tr><td></td><td>6</td><td></td></tr>
<tr><td>7</td><td></td><td>9</td></tr>
</table>

In this magic triangle each side adds up to 12.
Can you put in the missing numbers?

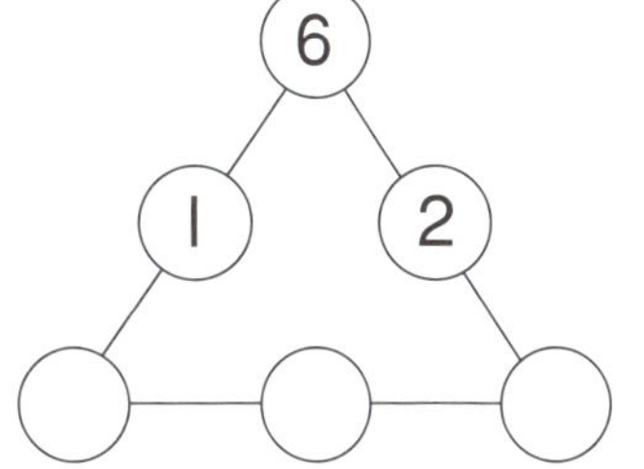

In this magic triangle each side adds up to 10.
Can you put in the missing numbers?

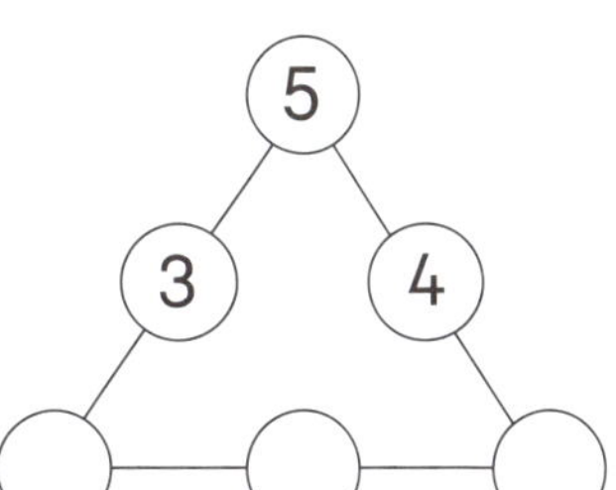

In this magic triangle each side adds up to 16.
Can you put in the missing numbers?

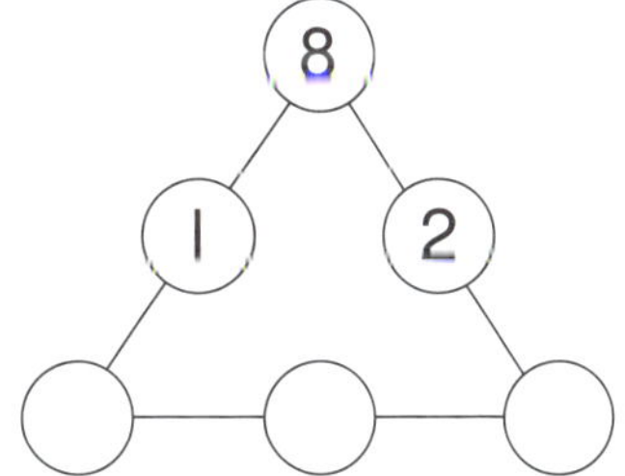

One way of solving a problem is called 'trial and error'.
You make a guess at the answer and then test it to see if it is right.
You can use this method to solve number puzzles.

Example:
We are two numbers that add up to 12 and multiply together to make 32.
What are we?

Think of some number pairs that add up to 12:

  1 + 11   2 + 10   3 + 9   4 + 8   5 + 7   6 + 6

and then test them to see which multiply to make 32:

  1 x 11 = 11   2 x 10 = 20   3 x 9 = 27   4 x 8 = 32

so the answer is 4 and 8.

You don't need to write all this out. You can do it in your head or make rough jottings.

Try to find the number pairs that answer these riddles:
We add up to 13 and multiply together to make 40.

_____________ and _____________

We add up to 12 and multiply together to make 35.

_____________ and _____________

We add up to 11 and multiply together to make 18.

_____________ and _____________

We add up to 14 and multiply together to make 48.

_____________ and _____________

Consecutive numbers are numbers that come next
to each other, such as:
3, 4, 5, or 8, 9, 10, or 32, 33, 34.
You could use trial and error on these problems –
but there might be a quicker way!

Example:
Find three consecutive numbers that add up to 33.

33 is near 30.
You know that 10 + 10 + 10 = 30, so the numbers must be near 10.

Try 9, 10 and 11.
They add up to only 30 so the numbers need to be a bit bigger.

Try 10, 11 and 12.
10 + 11 + 12 = 33, so you've found the answer!

Find three consecutive numbers that add up to 21.

__________   __________   __________

Find three consecutive numbers that add up to 48.

__________   __________   __________

Find three consecutive **odd** numbers that add up to 27.

__________   __________   __________

Find three consecutive **even** numbers that add up to 54.

__________   __________   __________

Can you find a quicker way to do these?

Some puzzles involve working out missing numbers. If only one number is missing there is usually only one answer.

17 + ? = 20   The answer must be 3.
30 − ? = 16   The answer must be 14.

See if you can work out the missing numbers in these puzzles.

25 + ____ = 34   35 − ____ = 21

____ + 16 = 29   ____ − 12 = 24

If there are several numbers missing there could be more than one right answer.

Choose three numbers from 1, 2, 3, 4 and 5 to fill in the blanks.

____ ____ + ____ = 17   The answer could be
                      13 + 4 = 17
                  or 14 + 3 = 17
                  or 15 + 2 = 17
                  or 12 + 5 = 17

See if you can find the missing numbers which will make these calculations right. Sometimes there is more than one answer. Use 1, 2, 3, 4 and 5.

____ ____ + ____ = 36   ____ ____ − ____ = 38

3____ + ____7 = 52   4____ − ____6 = 19

Can you split the set of numbers 1, 2, 3, 4, 5, 6, 7 and 8 into two sets of four, so that each set totals 18?

One way would be: 1, 2, 7, 8 and 3, 4, 5, 6

Can you find any other ways of doing it?

______, ______, ______, ______ and ______, ______, ______, ______.

______, ______, ______, ______ and ______, ______, ______, ______.

Can you split the set of numbers 1, 2, 3, 4, 5, 6, 7, 8 and 9 into three sets of three, so that each set totals 15?

_____, _____, _____ and _____, _____, _____ and _____, _____, _____.

Can you find another way of doing it?

_____, _____, _____ and _____, _____, _____ and _____, _____, _____.

Shape Symmetry

Each shape can be cut into two identical halves with a single straight line. Draw where the lines should go.

The first one is done for you.

Shape Symmetry

Can you draw in the missing bits to make these shapes symmetrical?

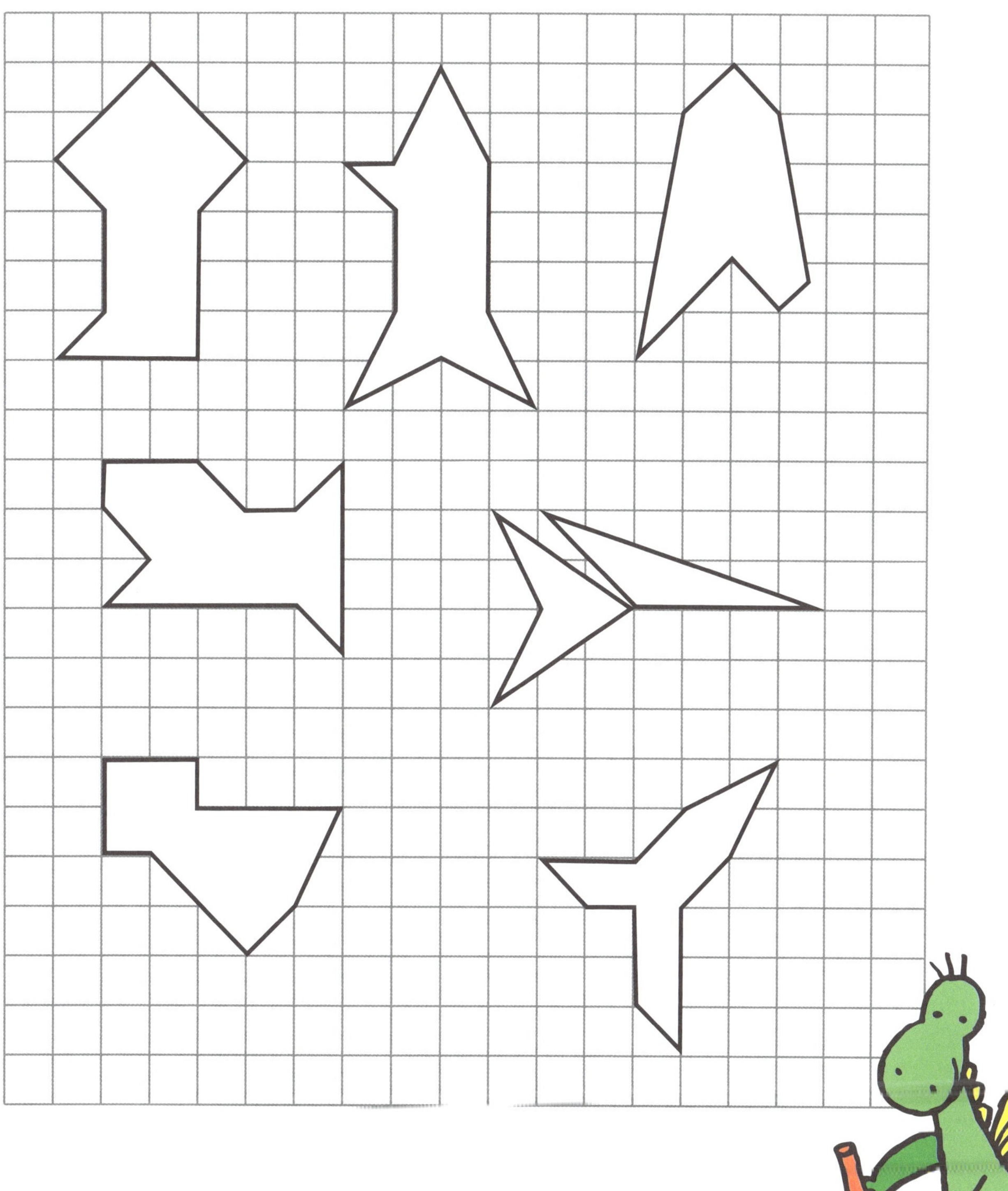

How many triangles can you see in this shape?

____

Jodie picked a solid shape out of the shape box at school.

She drew round each face of the shape.

What was the shape she picked? _______________________

Chris picked a different shape and drew round the faces.

What shape did he pick? _______________________

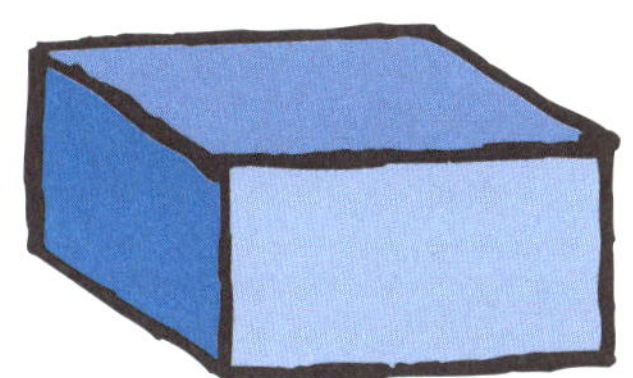 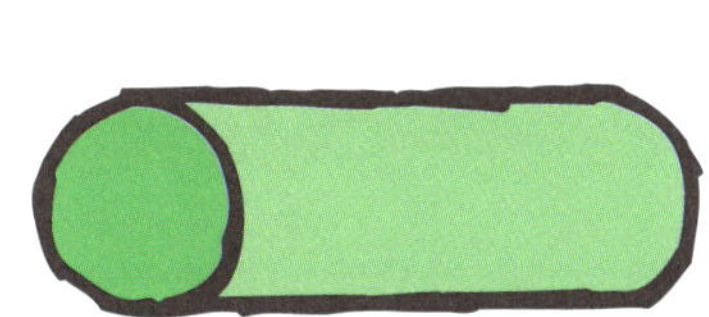 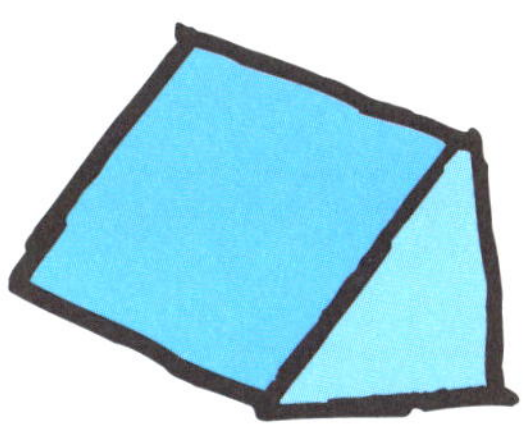 

Julie, James, Scott and Jessica had to describe the 3D shape they picked out of the box.

Can you identify the shapes from their descriptions?

Julie says, 'All of its faces are squares.'

____

James says, 'Two of its faces are circles.'

____

Scott says, 'Its faces are three pairs of rectangles.'

____

Julie says, 'It has one flat face and one curved face.'

____

Michael picked a triangular prism.
How would he describe it?

____

____

The children are making
a school magazine.

There are 32 children in the class.
They are working in pairs to write
articles for the magazine.
How many articles will be written?

____

The magazine has 8 pages.
How many articles will there be
on each page?

____

They need 4 sheets of paper for
each magazine. They decide to print
60 copies of the magazine.
How much paper will they need?

____

The school copier prints 40 sheets
of paper a minute.
How long will it take to print the magazines?

____

They decide to sell the magazine at the school fête for 50p a copy. How much money will they make if they sell them all?

____

They only sell 35 copies. How many copies are left unsold?

____

How much money do they make by selling 35 copies at 50p each?

____

They need £8 of the money to pay for printing the magazine. They give the rest to a charity. How much is there to give to charity?

____

Show your workings here:

Jodie, Michael, Natasha and Joe collect their sponsor money for the 50 lengths they have swum.

Jodie's grannny gives her 10p for each length she swam.

How much does she give Jodie? ______________

Michael's uncle gives him 5p for each length.

How much does he give him? ______________

Natasha's friend gives her 2p for each length.

How much does she give her? ______________

Joe's dad gives him £5 altogether.

How much is this for each length? ______________

Show your workings here:

How much did these people give them altogether?

Jodie's granny	£
Michael's uncle	£
Natasha's friend	£
Joe's dad	£ 5.00
Total	£

The four children finish collecting their sponsor money.
They sort the money out. Help them work out how much
money they have collected:

5 £2 coins = £________   20 £1 coins = £________

10 50p coins = £________   10 20p coins = £________

20 10p coins = £________   20 5p coins = £________

50 2p coins = £________   100 1p coins = £________

Altogether they have: £______________________________

They take the money to the bank to change into larger notes and coins.

They change the   5   £2 coins for __________ £5 notes.

They change the 20   £1 coins for __________ £10 notes.

They change the 10 50p coins for __________ £5 note.

They change the 10 20p coins for __________ £1 coins.

They change the 20 10p coins for __________ £1 coins.

They change the 20   5p coins for __________ £1 coin.

They change the 50   2p coins for __________ £1 coin.

They change the 100   1p coins for __________ £1 coin.

It's Sally's birthday soon. Her mum says that Sally can organise her party herself.

Sally invites 6 children to her party.
She makes up party bags of sweets for everyone.
The sweets in each bag cost 80p.
How much will all the bags cost?

____

She needs some music for the party.
She buys a CD for £12.50 and a cassette tape for £5.25.
How much did she spend?

____

She pays for the CD and tape with a £20 note.
How much change does she get?

____

She looks in the supermarket for drinks.
She could buy four 1 litre bottles of orange at £1.50 each,
or two 2 litre bottles for £2.75 each.
Which would be cheaper and by how much?

____

Sally decides to make up a fruit punch for the party.
Work out the total cost of the punch.

1 bottle of orange juice at £1.50	£
4 apples at 30p each	£
2 bottles of lemonade at £1.25 each	£
3 oranges at 25p each	£
2 lemons at 45p each	£
Total	£

How much change will she get from a £10 note?

____

Show your workings here:

The children help out at the shop.

Jodie's job is to weigh out the potatoes.

She puts the potatoes in bags.

Each bag can hold 5kg of potatoes.

How many bags will she need for 100kg of potatoes? _______________

Michael is helping with the apples.

Each apple weighs about 150g.

He has to put them in bags which hold 1kg.

Roughly how many apples will he put in each bag? _______________

Natasha is tying up the bags with string.

She needs 50cm of string for each bag.

How many bags can she tie up with 10m of string? _______________

Joe has the job of putting orange juice into bottles.

Each bottle holds $\frac{1}{2}$ litre.

How many bottles will he need for 20 litres of juice? _______________

Show your workings here:

The shopkeeper asks them to put out labels for the items on the shelves. Can you work out which label goes with which item?

Draw lines from the items to the correct labels.

Show your workings here:

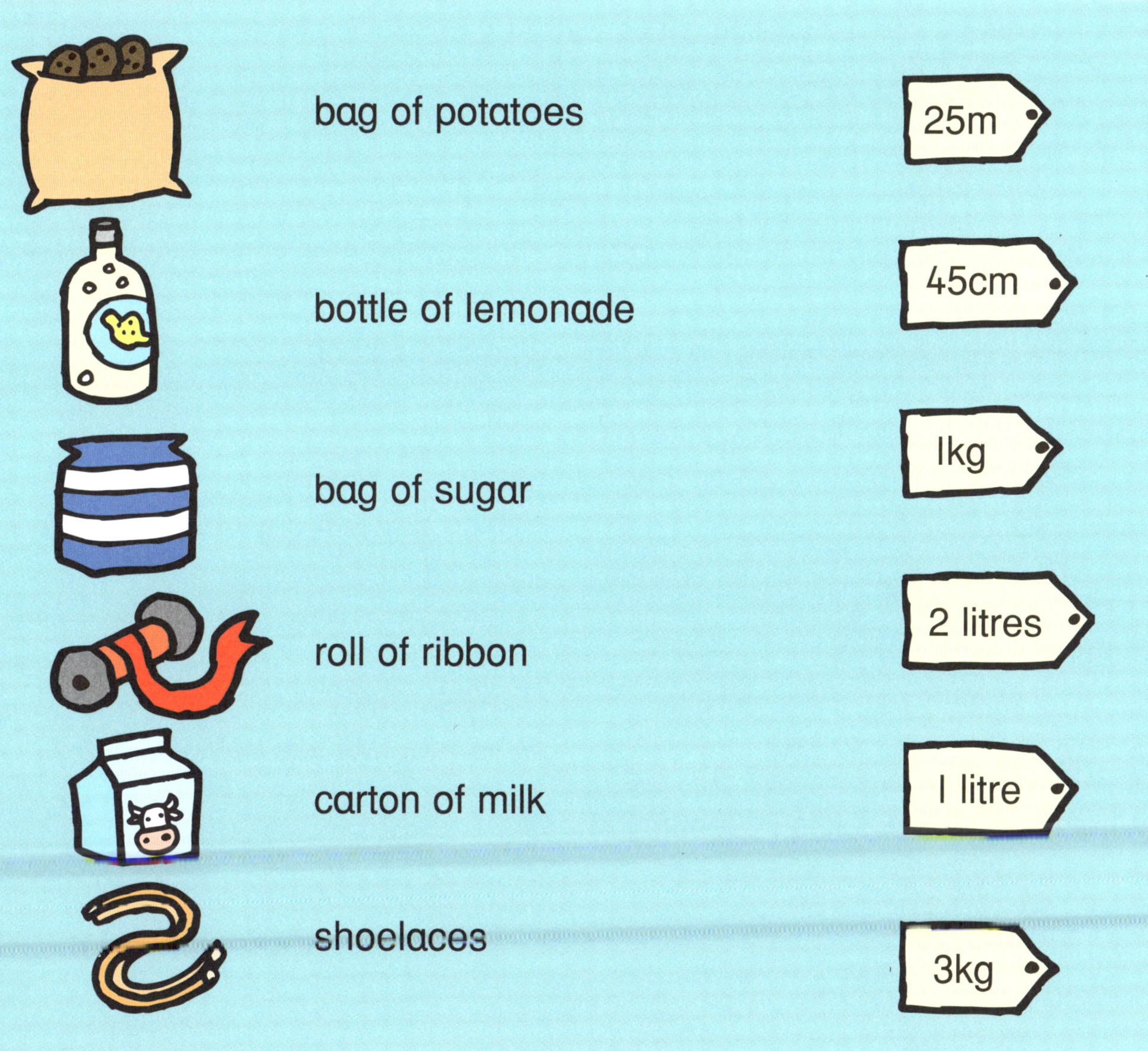

Here is another page from a calendar.

<table>
<tr><td colspan="7" align="center">January</td></tr>
<tr><td>Sunday</td><td>Monday</td><td>Tuesday</td><td>Wednesday</td><td>Thursday</td><td>Friday</td><td>Saturday</td></tr>
<tr><td></td><td></td><td>1</td><td>2</td><td>3</td><td>4</td><td>5</td></tr>
<tr><td>6</td><td>7</td><td>8</td><td>9</td><td>10</td><td>11</td><td>12</td></tr>
<tr><td>13</td><td>14</td><td>15</td><td>16</td><td>17</td><td>18</td><td>19</td></tr>
<tr><td>20</td><td>21</td><td>22</td><td>23</td><td>24</td><td>25</td><td>26</td></tr>
<tr><td>27</td><td>28</td><td>29</td><td>30</td><td>31</td><td></td><td></td></tr>
</table>

On which day does the month start?

____

On which day does the month finish?

____

How many days are there in the month?

____

What day of the week is 17 January?

____

Jessica goes on a two-week holiday on 10 January. On what day does she come back?

____

Which day is 4 days after Monday?

____

Tim's birthday is on 1 February. What day will this be?

____

The children at Hayland School are putting on a special evening.

They make up a programme for the different events.

Programme

7.30 pm	Choir
7.45 pm	Gym Display
8.05 pm	Recorder Group
8.15 pm	School Band
8.25 pm	Interval
8.45 pm	Play

Which item started at a quarter to eight?

____

Which item started at a quarter past eight?

____

What was on at 8.00 pm?

____

How long did the interval last?

____

The play lasted for half an hour. At what time did the evening finish?

____

Ben and Kevin are planning what TV programmes they will watch this evening, using this TV Guide.

TV Guide

DDCI		DDC2		ITB	
5.30	People Next Door	5.30	Near and Far	5.30	Weather Report
6.00	News	6.00	The Sampsons	5.40	Local News
6.15	Watchcat	6.30	Pulsebeat	6.15	THI Thursday
6.40	Top of the Flops	7.15	Changing Houses	7.00	Summerdale
7.30	Showtime	7.40	One Man and his Pig	7.30	Queen Street
8.15	Star Trip	8.10	Jasper Cabbage	8.00	Gardener's Life
10.05	Late News	8.45	Athletics	8.25	Badgerside
		9.40	News-square	9.15	North Park

What time does The Sampsons start?

____

How long does Pulsebeat last?

____

How long does Top of the Flops last?

____

How long does the film Star Trip last?

____

Which programme starts on DDC2 at 7.40?

____

What will be showing on ITB at 7.45?

____

At the end of Badgerside they turn to DDCI.
What programme is on?
How much have they missed of it?

____

On Saturday a group of children from Tinyville decide to go shopping in Bigtown.
They look at the bus timetable to plan their journey.

Bus Timetable

Tinyville to Bigtown			Bigtown to Tinyville		
Tinyville 8.15 am	9.10 am	10.22 am	Bigtown 1.00 pm	2.15 pm	3.32 pm
Midton 8.30 am	9.25 am	10.37 am	Fargate 1.20 pm	2.35 pm	3.52 pm
Fargate 8.40 am	9.35 am	10.47 am	Midton 1.30 pm	2.45 pm	4.02 pm
Bigtown 9.00 am	9.55 am	11.07 am	Tinyville 1.45 pm	3.00 pm	4.17 pm

What is the earliest bus they can catch from Tinyville?

____

What time would it get to Bigtown?

____

How long does the journey take from Tinyville to Bigtown?

____

How long is the journey from Midton to Fargate?

____

They want to be in Bigtown by 10.00 am. What time must they get the bus from Tinyville?

____

They arrive in Bigtown at 9.55 am. How long would they have in town if they caught the first bus back?

____

Their parents say they must be home by 3.30 pm.
What time must they get the bus in Bigtown?

____

They catch this bus but it is held up for 12 minutes by roadworks at Midton.
Will they get home in time?

____

The children are going to hold a
bring and buy sale at the school.

Joe brought a tray of cakes.
On the tray were 6 rows of 5 cakes.
How many cakes did he bring?

____

Tina brought 4 plates.
On each plate were 7 scones.
How many scones did she bring?

____

Jack brought 5 plates with 5 scones on each.
Did he bring more or less than Tina?

____

How many more or less?

____

The tables and chairs are set out in the hall.

There are:
5 tables with 4 chairs each
5 tables with 8 chairs each
5 tables with 9 chairs each

Were there enough chairs to seat 100 people?

____

Mary sold 24 cakes at 10p each.
How much money did she make?

____

Jane sold 15 buns at 20p each.
How much money did she make?

____

Mike brought sandwiches.
He brought 15 beef sandwiches, 23 ham sandwiches
and 25 cheese sandwiches.
How many sandwiches did he bring altogether?

Carla bought some cakes from the cake stall.

Scones were 16p each.
Apple tarts were 15p each.
Chocolate muffins were 14p each.

She bought 6 of one kind of cake.
She spent £1 and got 10p change.
Which kind of cake did she buy?

____

Tom and Emma are doing a survey of what games
children like to play in the playground.
There are 240 children in the school.

Half the children are boys and half are girls.
How many boys are there?

____

A quarter of the boys like to play football.
How many boys like to play football?

____

A third of the girls like to play football.
How many girls is this?

____

Half the children play on the field.
A quarter of the children prefer the playground.
The rest like to sit in the quiet area.
What fraction sit in the quiet area?

____

20 children are skipping.
5 of them are using blue ropes.
What fraction is this?

____

Tom and Emma ask a group of 12
children what their favourite item of
playground equipment is.
6 say the climbing frame.
4 say the scramble net.
2 say the sandpit.

What fraction preferred the
climbing frame?

____

What fraction preferred the
scramble net?

____

Tom and Emma asked 16 children if
they would like playtime to be longer.
Three-quarters of them said
they would.
How many children was this?

____

One-fifth of the children eat crisps at
playtime.
Two-fifths eat biscuits.
The rest eat fruit.
What fraction eat fruit?

____

Fill in the answers on this addition square.

+	1	2	3	4	5	6	7	8	9	10
1	2									
2		4	5	6	7	8	9	10	11	12
3			6	7	8	9	10	11	12	13
4				8	9	10	11	12	13	14
5	6				10	11				
6	7					12	13			
7	8						14	15		
8	9							16	17	
9	10								18	19
10	11	12	13	14	15	16	17	18	19	20

We call the number of times something happens "frequency".

How frequently does each group of answers appear?

Answer	Frequency
1–4	
5–8	
9–12	
13–16	
17–20	

Which answers have the highest frequency? _______________________

Why do you think these answers appear the most? _______________________

Which answers have the lowest frequency? _______________________

Why do you think these answers appear least? _______________________

Which number does not appear at all in the answers? _______________________

Why does this number not appear at all? _______________________

This block graph shows the number of television sets sold at a shop in one week.

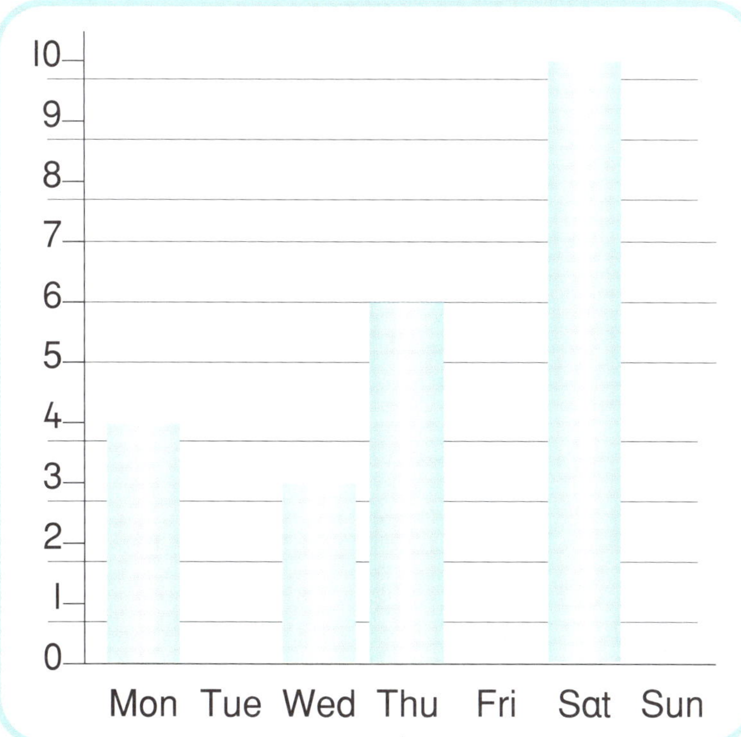

On Tuesday they sold half as many televisions as on Thursday.
Fill in the number of televisions sold on Tuesday.

On Friday they sold twice as many televisions as on Wednesday.
Fill in the graph to show how many televisions they sold on Friday.

On which day did they sell the most televisions? _______________________

What was the highest number of televisions sold? _______________________

On which day do you think the shop was closed? _______________________

Explain your answer. ____

____

The shop began the week with 50 televisions.
How many televisions do they still have left? _______________________

We use **tally marks** to count things.

1 = I	6 = ⊞ I
2 = II	7 = ⊞ II
3 = III	8 = ⊞ III
4 = IIII	9 = ⊞ IIII
5 = ⊞	10 = ⊞ ⊞ and so on.

Count the tally marks and write how many there are.

⊞ ⊞ II = __________________

⊞ I = __________________

⊞ ⊞ ⊞ ⊞ ⊞ = __________________

⊞ ⊞ ⊞ II = __________________

Count the vehicles in the traffic jam.

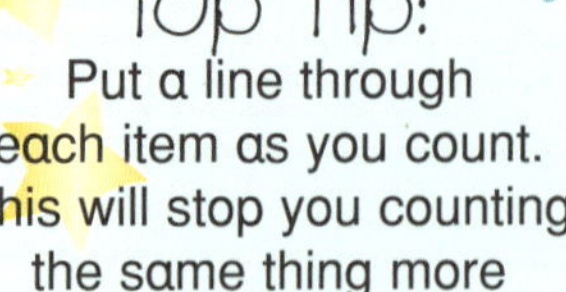

Lorry	__________________
Car	__________________
Motorbike	__________________
Total	__________________

Use tally marks to count each group of items.

fish ___________________ octopus ___________________

starfish ___________________ sea snail ___________________

house ___________________ window ___________________

chimney-pot ___________________ door ___________________

This is a bar chart for the number of hours a family spent watching television over a two-week holiday.

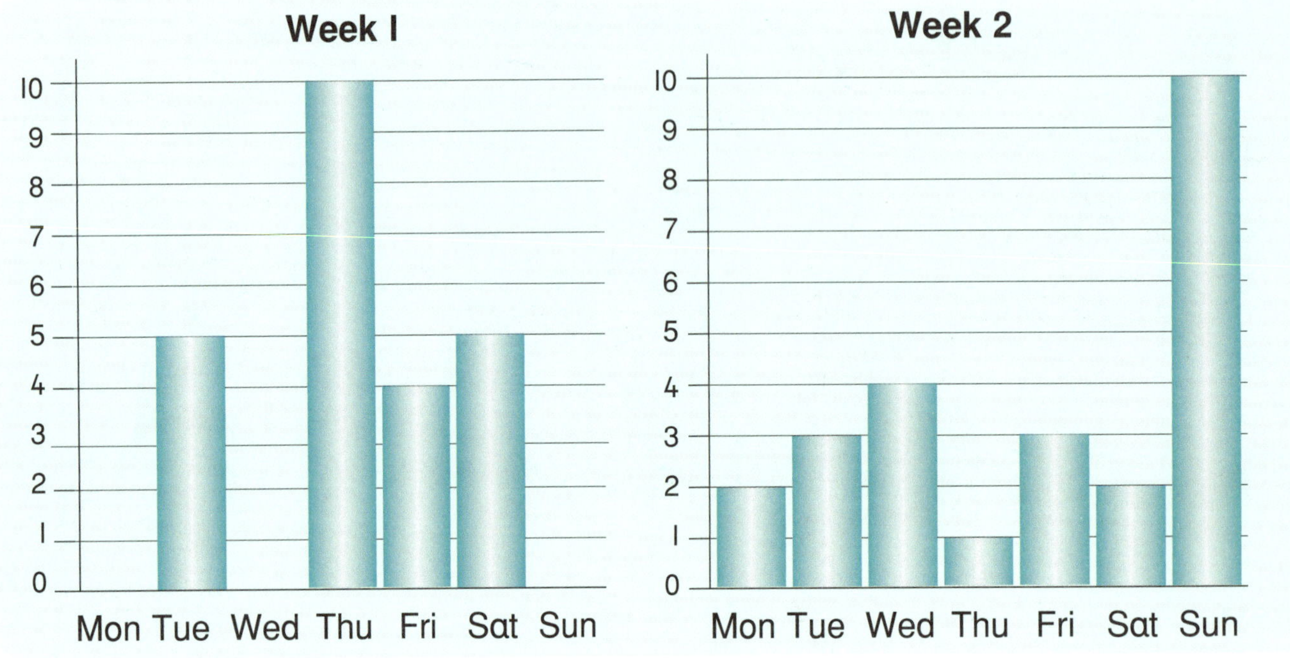

Complete the bar chart using this information.
The family watched twice as much television on the first Monday than on the second. The family watched half as much television on the first Wednesday than on the second.

Look at the bar chart and then answer these questions.

Two days of the holidays had very bad weather. On which days do you think the weather was worst?
Explain why you think this.

____

____

____

____

What day during the holiday do you think the family went out all day?
Explain why you think this.

____

____

____

Which week did the family spend the most amount of time watching television? _______________________

Bar charts

Use the information in this chart to complete the bar chart.

Time	Cars Washed
8:00–9:00	9
9:00–10:00	4
10:00–11:00	3
11:00–12:00	8
12:00–1:00	6
1:00–2:00	3
2:00–3:00	2
3:00–4:00	3
4:00–5:00	1
5:00–6:00	10

Top Tip: The title of a chart tells what it is about. Each axis measures something. On this one the side axis measures how many cars; the bottom axis measures time.

Give your chart a title. Name each axis.

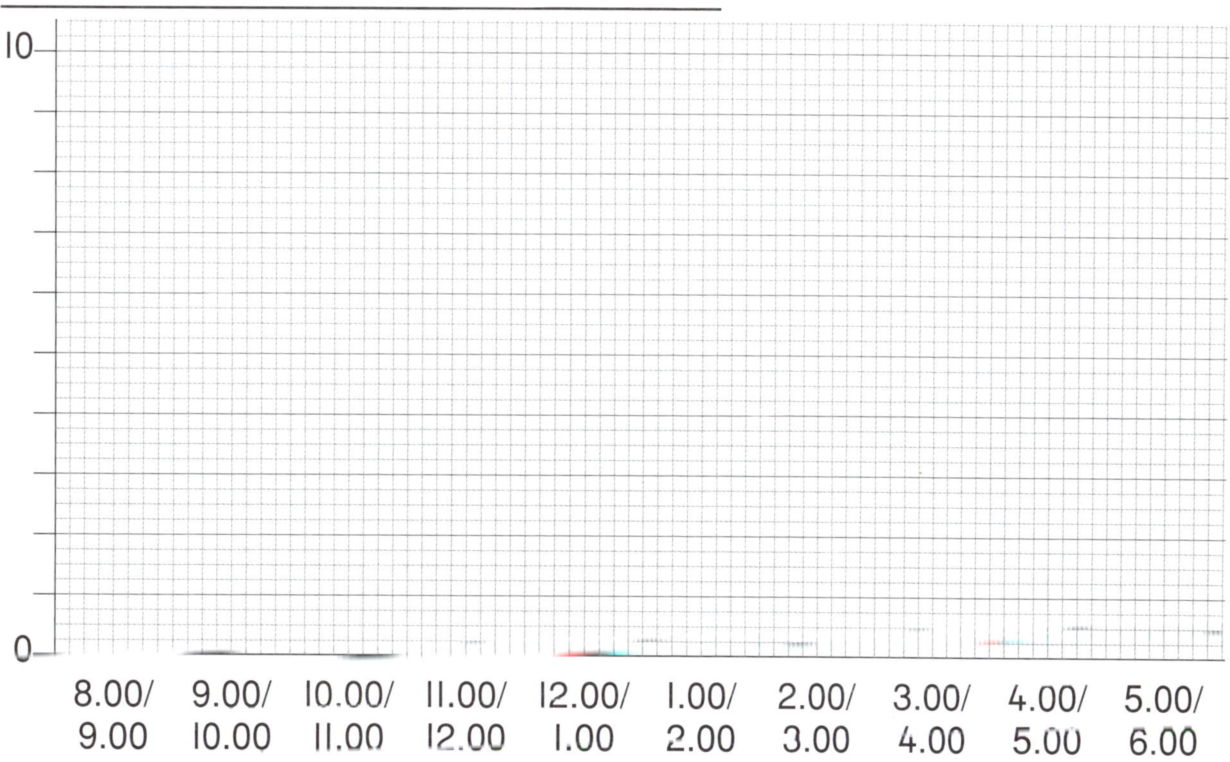

Use this information to complete the bar chart.

Time	Buses
8:00–9:00	10
9:00–10:00	5
10:00–11:00	3
11:00–12:00	2
12:00–1:00	6
1:00–2:00	4
2:00–3:00	3
3:00–4:00	2
4:00–5:00	3
5:00–6:00	10

Give your chart a title. Name each axis.

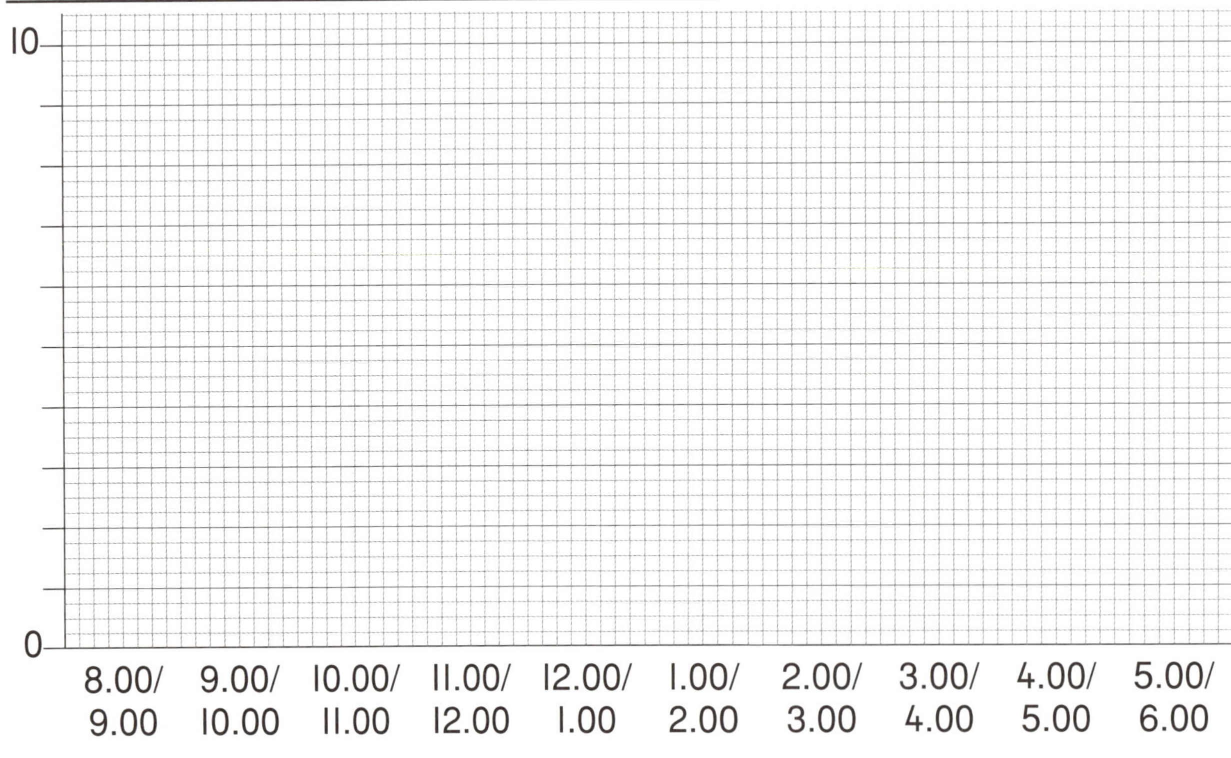

When does the greatest number of buses travel? ___________________

Why do you think there are more buses at these times? ___________________

Bar charts and pictograms

A pictogram is a way of showing information.
It uses pictures to represent things.
This picture ⛹ means I person.

How many people do you think this picture shows? _______________________

Look at this pictogram. Write down next to the pictogram
the number of people who go swimming each day.

Days	Swimming	How many?
Mon	⛹ ⛹ ⛹ ⛹ ⛹ ⛹ ⛹ ⛹	
Tue	⛹ ⛹ ⛹ ⛹ ⛹ ⛹ ⛹ ⛹ ⛹ ⛹ ⛹	
Wed	⛹ ⛹ ⛹ ⛹ ⛹ ⛹ ⛹	
Thu	⛹ ⛹ ⛹ ⛹ ⛹ ⛹	
Fri	⛹ ⛹ ⛹ ⛹ ⛹	
Sat	⛹ ⛹ ⛹ ⛹ ⛹ ⛹ ⛹ ⛹	
Sun	⛹ ⛹ ⛹ ⛹ ⛹ ⛹ ⛹ ⛹ ⛹ ⛹	

What day did the greatest number of children go swimming? _______________

What day did half that number go swimming? _______________

What day did the least number of children go swimming? _______________

Sometimes a pictogram is used to stand for
a number of people, things or events.

This cake  stands for 10 cakes.

How many cakes does each of these pictograms stand for?

 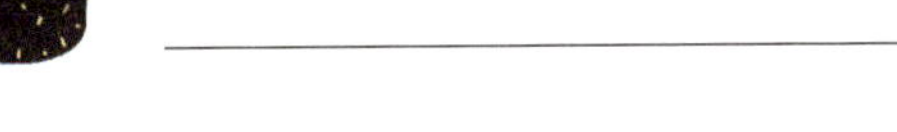

 ___________________________

This car means that 10 cars have been sold.
How many cars did this company sell each month?

Month	Sales	How many?
Jan	🚗🚗🚗	
Feb	🚗🚗	
Mar	🚗🚗🚗🚗🚗🚗🚙	
Apr	🚗	
May	🚗🚗	
Jun	🚙	
Jul	🚗🚗🚗🚙	
Aug	🚗🚗🚗🚗🚗🚙	
Sep	🚗🚗🚗🚗🚙	
Oct	🚗🚙	
Nov	🚙	
Dec	🚗🚗🚙	

Pictograms

This pictogram stands for the number of hot school meals eaten in a year.

⊞ = 20 plates

Here is a list of all the meals eaten each month.

Use the symbol above to show the information as a pictogram.

	Meals Eaten	**Pictogram**
January	卌 卌 卌 卌 卌 卌 卌 卌 卌	
February	卌 卌 卌 卌 卌 卌 卌	
March	卌 卌 卌 卌 卌 卌	
April	卌 卌 卌 卌 卌	
May	卌 卌 卌 卌	
June	卌 卌 卌 卌	
July	卌 卌	
August		
September	卌 卌 卌 卌 卌 卌 卌 卌	
October	卌 卌 卌 卌 卌 卌 卌 卌 卌 卌	
November	卌 卌 卌 卌 卌 卌 卌 卌 卌 卌 卌	
December	卌 卌 卌 卌 卌 卌 卌 卌 卌 卌 卌 卌 卌	

Why does the number go up during December? _______________________

What month do you think school is closed? _______________________

Explain your answer. _______________________

Which way of showing the information is easiest to understand? _______________________

Explain your answer. _______________________

When we have a large number of items to count,
we can use a pictogram to represent more than 1 of each item.

This pictogram  represents 20 ferry crossings.

How many pictograms represent:

60 ferry crossings	__________	140 ferry crossings	__________
100 ferry crossings	__________	160 ferry crossings	__________
120 ferry crossings	__________	180 ferry crossings	__________

We can use part of a pictogram to represent a number, too:

This pictogram  represents 20 ferry crossings.

This pictogram represents 15 ferry crossings – it is $\frac{3}{4}$ of the size so it represents $\frac{3}{4}$ of the number.

This pictogram represents 10 ferry crossings – it is half the size so it represents half the number.

This pictogram represents 5 ferry crossings – it is $\frac{1}{4}$ of the size so it represents $\frac{1}{4}$ of the number.

How many pictograms represent:

15 ferry crossings	__________	40 ferry crossings	__________
25 ferry crossings	__________	110 ferry crossings	__________

Write how many ferry crossings there are each month in the last column of the table. Then read the frequency table to answer the questions below.

Month	Number of ferry crossings	
January		
February		
March		
April		
May		
June		
July		
August		
September		
October		
November		
December		

Which month was quietest?____

Which month was busiest?____

Which month has half as many crossings as August?__________________

Which two months had the same number of crossings?__________________

Bar graph scales

Use this frequency chart to draw a bar chart.

What is the best increase for each interval?

Remember that the interval is how much the numbers along the side go up by.

Theme park visitors for this year	
Month	**Thousand of visitors**
January	5
February	10
March	20
April	35
May	45
June	60
July	60
August	60
September	50
October	45
November	10
December	5

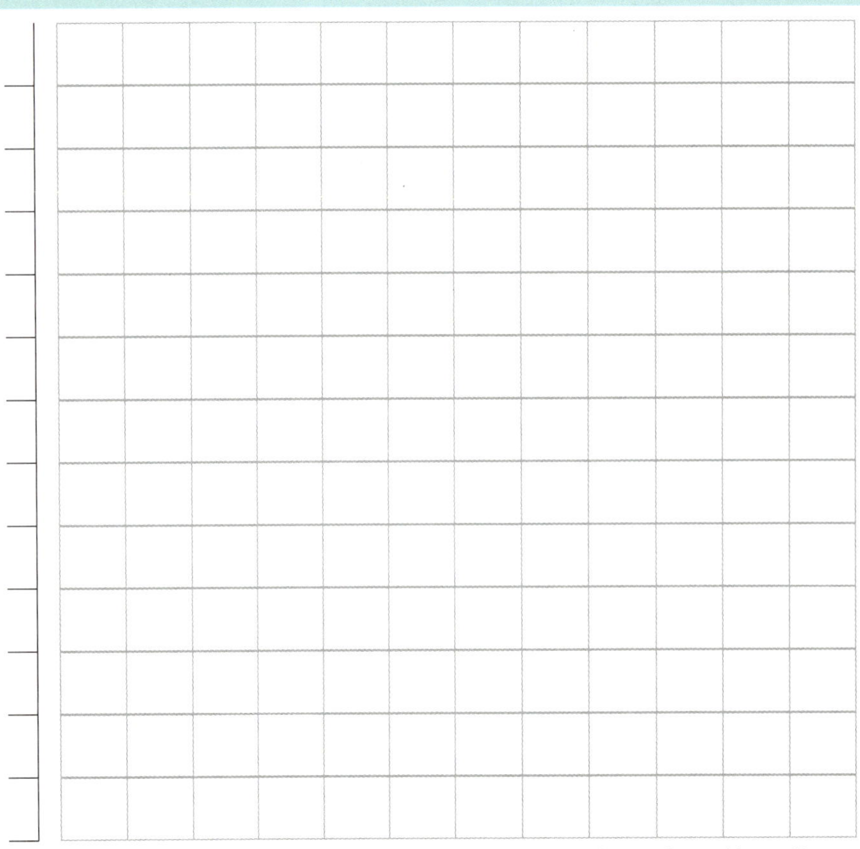

Bar graph scales

Look at the information below. It shows the number of computers sold during a year.

	Hundreds
Jan	33
Feb	29
Mar	22
Apr	17
May	12
Jun	14
Jul	19
Aug	23
Sep	24
Oct	28
Nov	30
Dec	39

Look at the computer sales carefully and the graph template shown below. Decide on the best interval to show all the information. It may help if you think of the numbers as being just below or just above the nearest multiple of 5. (For example, 23 is nearly 25.)

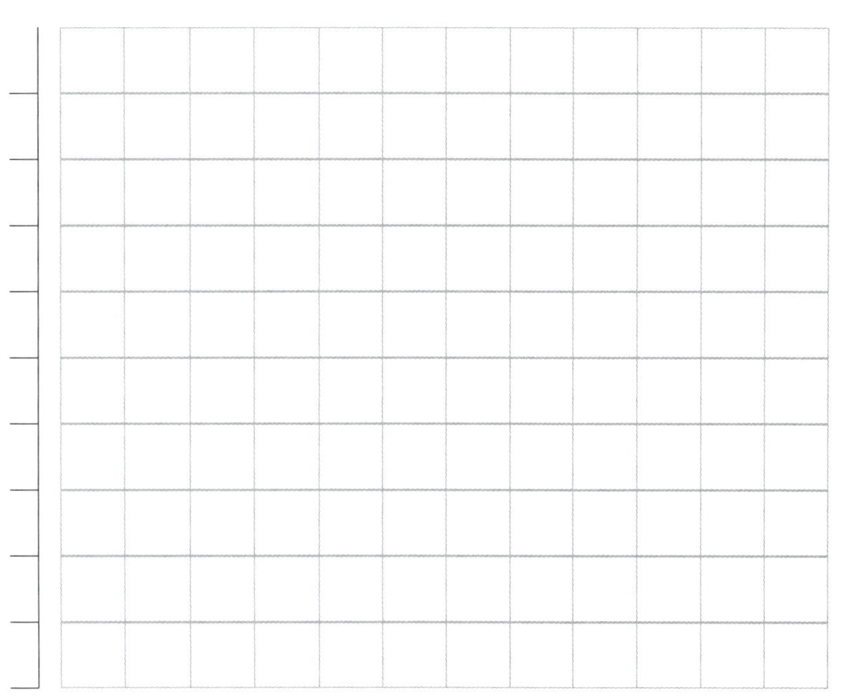

Why do you think they sold more computers during December and January?

____

____

____

____

Look at the information shown in this graph.

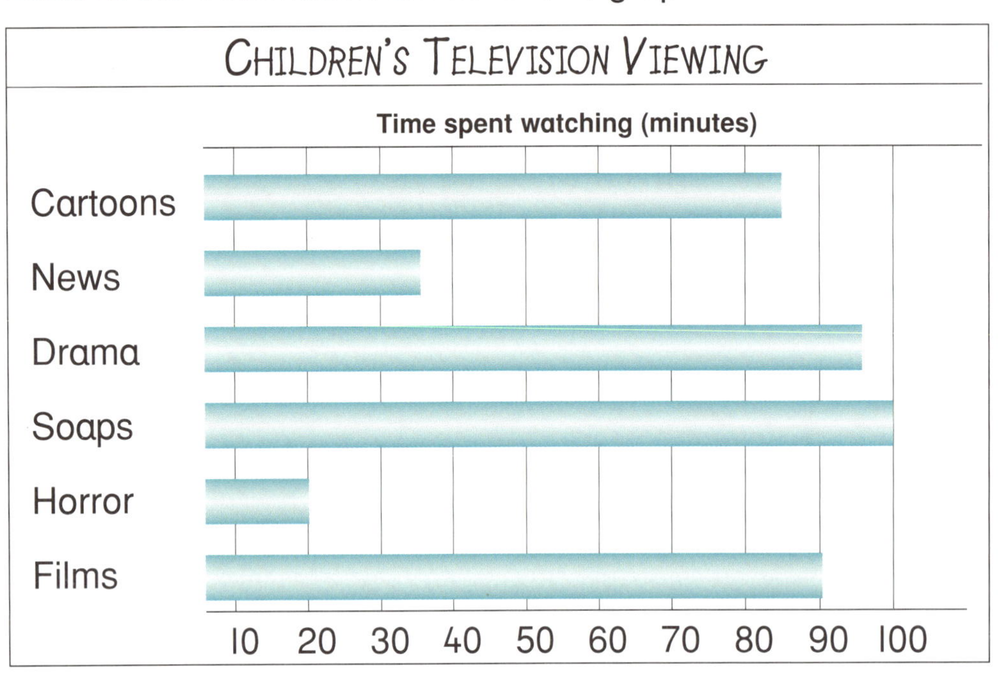

What did children spend most of their time watching?

____

How many programmes were watched for longer than an hour?

____

What is the least watched type of programme type?

____

Which type of programme is watched for $1\frac{1}{2}$ hours?

____

Which type of programme is watched for 1 hour longer than the news?

____

If you wanted to put an advert on during a programme, which programme would you choose? Explain your answer.

____

Look at cooking times shown on this chart.

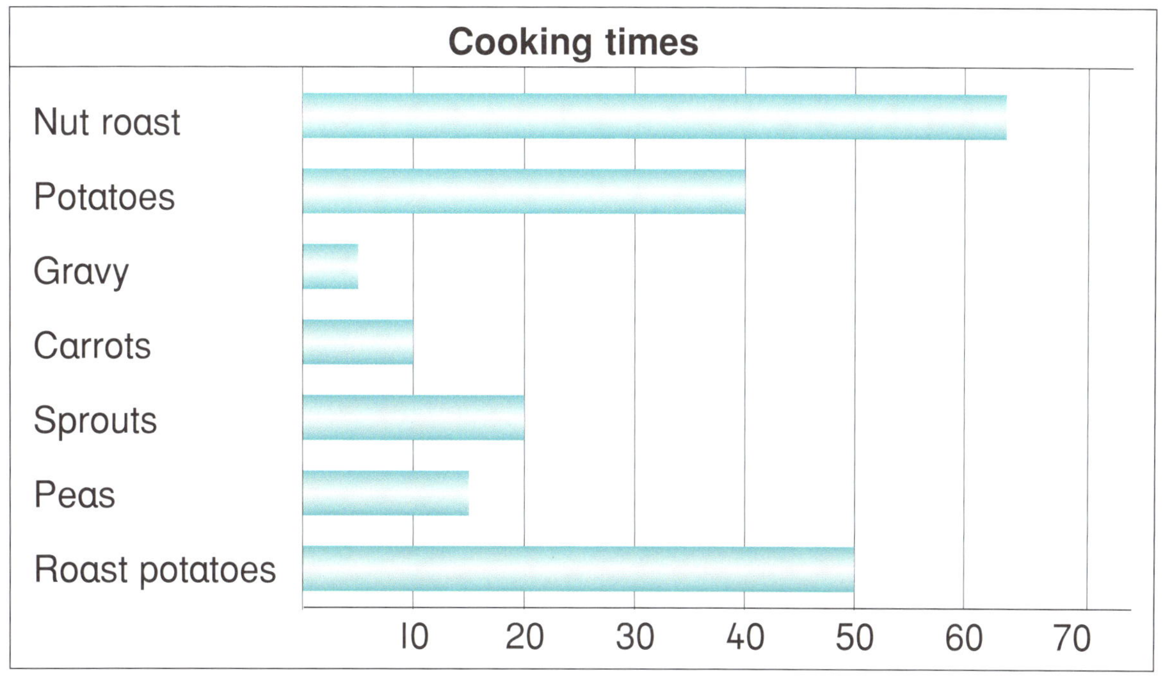

Which food takes the longest to prepare? _______________________

Imagine you had to prepare this meal for your family.

If the meal had to be ready at 1:00 in the afternoon what times would you have to start cooking each piece of food to make sure they were all ready at 1 o'clock?

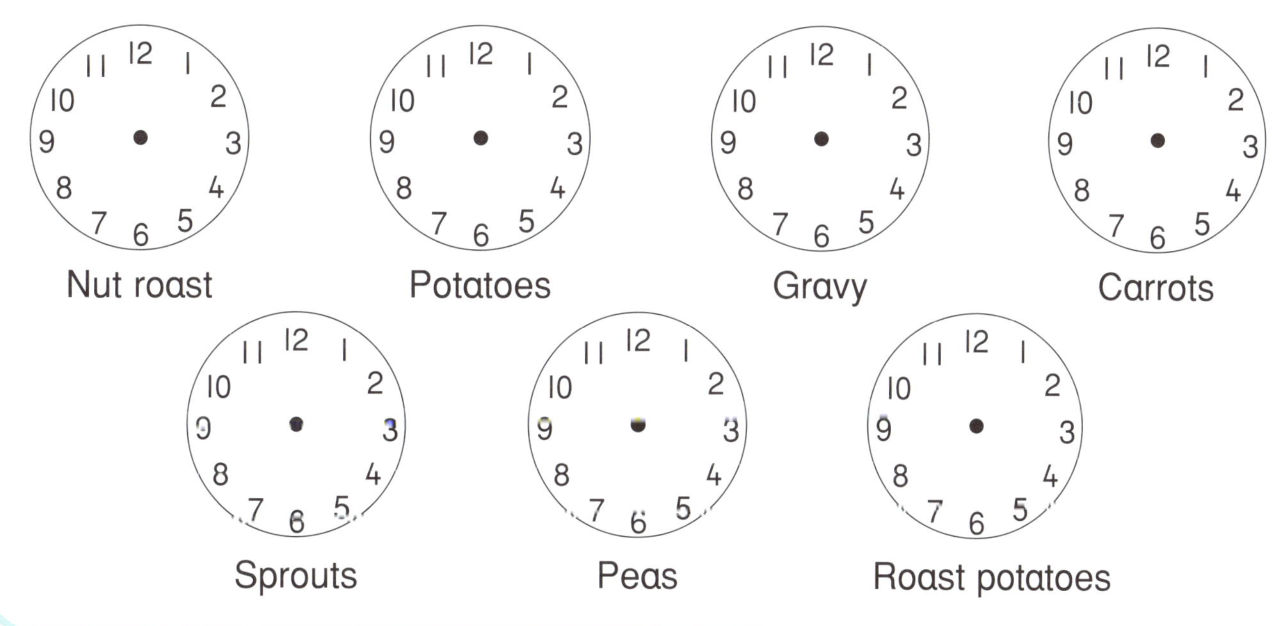

I conducted a survey among my friends.

I wanted to find out what they like to do at the weekend.

Collecting data and recording it in a frequency table

I gave them a list of activities. Then I ticked off the activities they liked.

	Computer games	Shopping	Swimming	Watching TV
Jenny	✔	✔	✔	
Mel		✔	✔	
Martin	✔	✔		
Jerry	✔		✔	
Charlie	✔		✔	✔
Vicci				

Use this frequency table to find out what your friends like to do.

Name	Computer games	Shopping	Swimming	Watching TV

Presenting the data

I drew a bar chart to show the results of the survey.

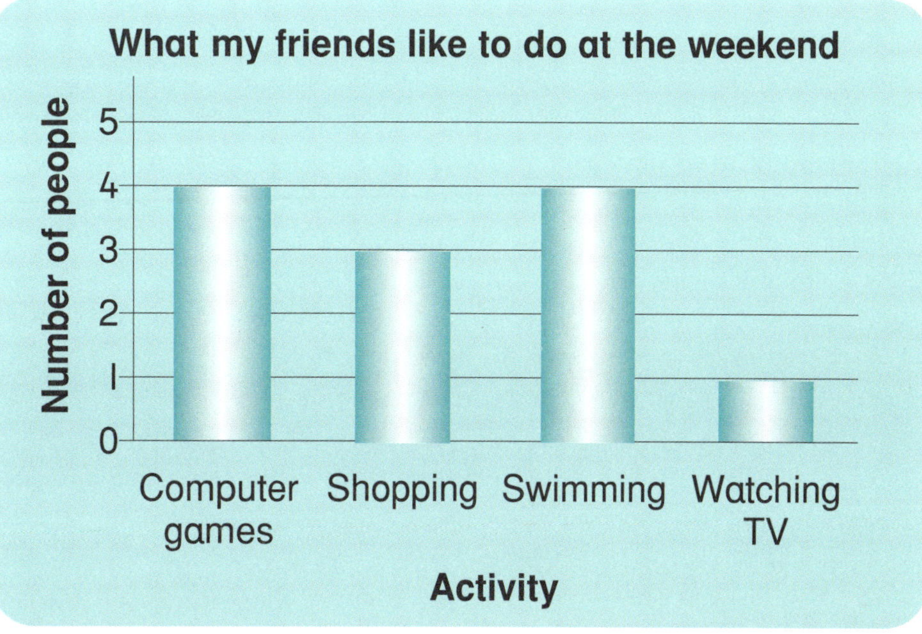

Which two activities are the most popular?________________________

Which activity was the least popular?________________________

Now draw a bar chart for **your** survey.

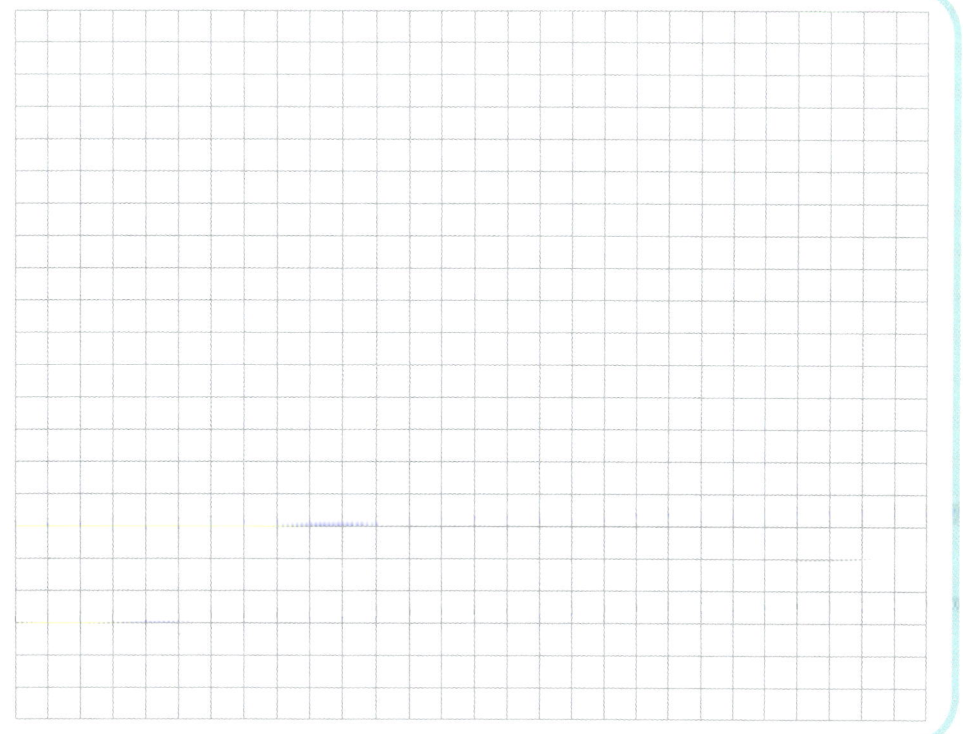

page 4
78 + 5 = 83, 124 + 8 = 132, 235 + 7 = 242, 337 + 4 = 341.
85 + 30 = 115, 124 + 40 = 164, 68 + 50 = 118, 95 + 20 = 115

page 5
0, 5, 10, 15, 20, 25, 30, 35, 40, 45.
8, 13, 18, 23, 28, 33, 38, 43, 48, 53.
6, 11, 16, 21, 26, 31, 36, 41, 46, 51.
9, 14, 19, 24, 29, 34, 39, 44, 49, 54.
7, 12, 17, 22, 27, 32, 37, 42, 47, 52.
3 + 5 + 7 + 5 + 2 = (3 + 7) + (5 + 5) + 2 = 10 + 10 + 2 = 20 + 2 = 22.
6 + 3 + 4 + 1 + 7 = (6 + 4) + (3 + 7) + 1 = 10 + 10 + 1 = 20 + 1 = 21.

page 6
56 + 9 = 65, 74 + 19 = 93, 87 + 29 = 116, 63 + 39 =102, 134 + 9 = 143,
236 + 19 = 255, 323 + 29 = 352, 354 + 39 = 393.
85 + 11 = 96, 64 + 21 = 85, 58 + 31 = 89, 72 + 41 = 113, 134 + 11 = 145,
435 + 21 = 456, 546 + 31 = 577, 227 + 41 = 268.
76 − 9 = 67, 86 − 19 = 67, 154 − 29 = 125, 345 − 39 = 306,
86 − 11 = 75, 93 − 21 = 72, 386 − 31 = 355, 556 − 41 = 515.

page 7
17 + 35 → 17 + 85 = 52, 62, 72, 82, 92, 102.
87 − 34 → 87 − 84 = 53, 43, 33, 23, 13, 3.
500 + 300 = 800, 5000 + 3000 = 8000, 700 − 200 = 500,
7000 − 2000 = 5000.

+	1	2	3	4	5	6	7	8	9	10
1	2	3	4	5	6	7	8	9	10	11
2	3	4	5	6	7	8	9	10	11	12
3	4	5	6	7	8	9	10	11	12	13
4	5	6	7	8	9	10	11	12	13	14
5	6	7	8	9	10	11	12	13	14	15
6	7	8	9	10	11	12	13	14	15	16
7	8	9	10	11	12	13	14	15	16	17
8	9	10	11	12	13	14	15	16	17	18
9	10	11	12	13	14	15	16	17	18	19
10	11	12	13	14	15	16	17	18	19	20

page 8
20 ÷ 2 = 10, 16 ÷ 2 = 8, 40 ÷ 5 = 8, 25 ÷ 5 = 5, 40 ÷ 10 = 4,
60 ÷ 10 = 6.
9, 7, 7, 3, 5, 8

page 9
Half: 12 = 6, 8 = 4, 20 = 10.
Double: 6 = 12, 4 = 8, 10 = 20.
14 x 2 → 20 x 2: 28, 30, 32, 34, 36, 38, 40.
Half 28 → 40: 14, 15, 16, 17, 18, 19, 20.

page 10
14 + 16 = 30, 18 + 22 = 40, 35 + 25 = 60, 37 + 23 = 60, 49 + 21 = 70,
48 + 22 = 70, 38 + 32 = 70, 57 + 33 = 90, 63 + 27 = 90,
24 + 66 = 90. They are all multiples of 10.
95 + 5 = 100, 23 + 77 = 100, 60 + 40 = 100. 98 + 2 = 100,
20 + 80 = 100, 88 + 12 = 100, 59 + 41 = 100, 51 + 49 = 100,
40 + 60 = 100, 48 + 52 = 100.

page 11
8 x 2 = 16, 45 ÷ 5 = 9, 6 x 5 = 30, 18 ÷ 2 = 9, 9 x 10 = 90, 50 ÷ 10 = 5,
5 x 3 = 15, 25 ÷ 5 = 5, 2 x 7 = 14, 60 ÷ 10 = 6, 23 x 10 = 230,
350 ÷ 10 = 35, 25 x 2 = 50, 34 ÷ 2 = 17, 30 x 10 = 300, 100 ÷ 2 = 50,
14 x 2 = 28, 650 ÷ 10 = 65, 3 x 100 = 300, 700 ÷ 100 = 7.

page 12
LEARNING THESE FACTS HELPS TO SOLVE
HARDER PROBLEMS

page 13
40 + 30 = 70, 50 + 90 = 140, 60 + 70 = 130, 70 + 80 = 150,
500 + 600 = 1100, 600 + 900 = 1500, 800 + 400 = 1200,
400 + 300 = 700, 60 − 10 = 50, 90 − 30 = 60, 80 − 40 = 40,
100 − 30 = 70, 600 − 400 = 200, 1200 − 300 = 900, 700 − 100 = 600,
1500 − 800 = 700.
60 = 100 − 40
80 = 30 + 50
500 = 900 − 400
800 = 1200 − 400
1400 = 600 + 800

page 14
Ring: 3 + 7, 6 + 4, 5 + 5, 2 + 8
Ring: 40 + 60, 20 + 80, 30 + 70, 90 + 10
Ring: 38 + 62, 18 + 82, 53 + 47, 24 + 76
45 + 55, 56 + 44, 37 + 63, 81 + 19, 46 + 54, 34 + 66, 71 + 29

page 15
500, 300, 800, 50, 250, 350.
The hidden number is 74

page 16
20, 50, 200, 120, 51, 67, 100

page 17
11 r1, 7 r1, 6 r1, 13 r1, 6 r4, 8 r3, 9 r2, 8 r1, 6 r2
2 teams with 2 left over
5 boxes with 2 left over
4 crates with 5 left over

page 18
£3.50, £4.50, £2.50, £2.25, £3.50, £4.25, £3.20, £6.40, £9.75, £3.20,
£4.30, £6.40.
£3.20, £2.50, £2.50

page 19
4 x 4 to 10 x 4: 16, 20, 24, 28, 32, 36, 40
4 x 3 to 10 x 3: 12, 15, 18, 21, 24, 27, 30

page 20
7 x 2 = 14, 6 x 3 = 18, 8 x 4 = 32, 10 x 5 = 50, 9 x 10 = 90.
Pick key 15.

page 21
THE TREASURE IS HIDDEN FOUR TIMES SIX PACES NORTH
OF THE OLD STATUE.

page 22
4 x 3 = 12, then x 2 = 24,
5 x 3 = 15, then x 2 = 30,
6 x 3 = 18, then x 2 = 36,
7 x 3 = 21, then x 2 = 42,
8 x 3 = 24, then x 2 = 48,
9 x 3 = 27, then x 2 = 54,
10 x 3 = 30, then x 2 = 60.
6 x 11 = 60 + 6 = 66,
9 x 11 = 90 + 9 = 99,
11 x 11 = 110 + 11 = 121,
14 x 11 = 140 + 14 = 154,
15 x 11 = 150 + 15 = 165,
20 x 11 = 200 + 20 = 220,
19 x 11 = 190 + 19 = 209

page 23
6 x 9 = 54, 7 x 9 = 63, 9 x 9 = 81, 11 x 9 = 99, 15 x 9 = 135,
20 x 9 = 180, 25 x 9 = 225

page 24
13 x 10 to 80 x 10 = 130, 140, 150, 160, 170, 180, 190, 200.
400, 450, 500, 550, 600, 650, 700, 750, 800.
320, 240, 480, 530, 1350, 2460.
800, 1500, 2300, 5400, 6800, 12 500.

Answers

page 25
38 boxes, 47 boxes, 156 boxes, 260 boxes.
38 lorries, 29 lorries, 86 lorries, 100 lorries.

page 26
The correct answers are: 425 − 38 = 387, 347 − 85 = 262,
531 − 143 = 388.
350 ÷ 5 = 70, 156 ÷ 3 = 52, 164 ÷ 4 = 41

page 27
The first two and the last calculations are wrong.
24 + 30 + 16 = 83, 56 + 38 = 121, 356 + 462 = 889 are all wrong.

page 28

page 29

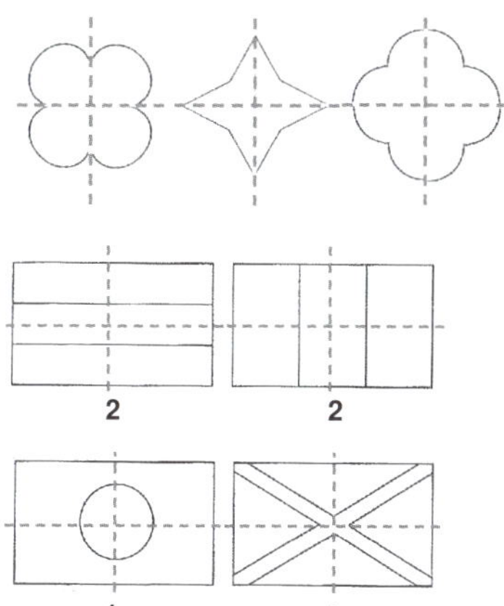

page 30
A E G C B F D H

page 31
A *square* has 4 sides and 4 right angles. 0 angle is larger than a
right angle. 0 angle is smaller than a right angle. It has 4 vertices.
A *rectangle* has 4 sides and 4 right angles. 0 angle is larger than a
right angle. 0 angle is smaller than a right angle. It has 4 vertices.
This *triangle* has 3 sides and 0 right angles. 0 angle is larger than a
right angle. 3 angles are smaller than a right angle. It has 3 vertices.
A *circle* has 0 sides and 0 right angles. 0 angle is larger than a right
angle. 0 angle is smaller than a right angle. It has 0 vertices.
A *parallelogram* has 4 sides and 0 right angles. 2 angles are larger
than a right angle. 2 angles are smaller than a right angle. It has 4
vertices.

This *pentagon* has 5 sides and 0 right angles. 5 angles are larger
than a right angle. 0 angle is smaller than a right angle. It has 5
vertices.
A *hexagon* has 6 sides and 0 right angles. 6 angles are larger than
a right angle. 0 angle is smaller than a right angle. It has 6 vertices.
An *octagon* has 8 sides and 0 right angles. 8 angles are larger than
a right angle. 0 angle is smaller than a right angle. It has 8 vertices.

page 32
A. Circle
B. Equilateral triangle
C. Semi-circle
D. Triangle
E. Square
F. Isosceles triangle
G. Pentagon
H. Quadrilateral
I. Rectangle
J. Hexagon
K. Heptagon
L. Regular hexagon

page 33
Cuboid 6, 12, 8
Triangular prism 5, 9, 6
Cube 6, 12, 8
Tetrahedron 4, 6, 4

page 34
16cm
8 x 3cm = 24cm; the hexagon is bigger, it has a perimeter of
6 x 3cm = 18cm
Use a ruler to measure each perimeter carefully.

page 35
A 8cm², B 12cm², C 2cm², D 15cm², E 12cm², F 10cm², G 16cm²

page 36
A 12cm, 8cm²
B 14cm, 12cm²
C 18cm, 14cm²
D 16cm, 7cm²
E 16cm, 16cm²
F 20cm, 24cm²

page 37
A 12cm, 6cm²
B 14cm, 10cm²
C 18cm, 11cm²
D 24cm, 15cm²
E 24cm, 22cm²
F 20cm, 16cm²

page 38
A 12cm³; B 18cm³; C 24cm³; D 40cm³; E 6cm³; F 32cm³

page 39
A 8cm³; B 4cm³; C 8cm³; D 12cm³; E 5cm³; F 9cm³; G 6cm³;
H 10cm³; I 13cm³

page 40
1 measuring jug, ml
2 foot measure/ruler, cm
3 scales, g
4 tape measure, m/cm

page 41
km; m; kg; g; ml; g; cm or mm; mm; litre; mm

page 42
There are 100 centimetres in a metre; there are 50 centimetres in half a metre
75cm; 38cm; 134cm; 154cm; 98cm
1.42m; 1.54m; 1.98m; 0.98m; 1.34m

page 43
350cm = 3.5m
1.36m = 1 m 36cm
1m 5cm = 1.05m
7.02m = 7 metres 2cm
149cm = 1m 49cm
1m 54cm = 1.54m
0.95m = 95cm
950cm = 9.5m
1.5m = 150cm

page 44
500ml, 1000ml, 100ml
B, C
500ml, 250ml, 150ml, 900ml, 750ml, 850ml

page 45
$\frac{1}{4}$ kg, 1$\frac{3}{4}$ kg, 2$\frac{1}{2}$ kg; 1$\frac{1}{2}$ kg; 2$\frac{1}{4}$ kg, 1$\frac{3}{4}$ kg

page 46
A 85mm
B 10.5cm
C 300ml
D 450ml
E 40kg
F 70kg

page 47
A 340cm; 150cm; 430cm; 340cm
B 50cm; 10cm; 600cm; 600cm
C 200g; 1200g; 4600g; 5800g
D 100g; 0g; 4300g; 1000g

page 48
Wednesday; 17 November; Yes, it is a week day; 6 December; 25 days; 24 October

page 49
Monster Trucks starts at 5:20; *Aussie Street* begins at 5:35; *Ward 7* lasts 40 minutes; *Cartoon Mystery* is 15 minutes longer than the *News*; 1 hour and 35 minutes longer.
Revenge of the Turtle: 4:00 pm to 5:29 pm
Haunted Castle IV: 6:00 pm to 7:58 pm
Mad for Maths III: 8 pm to 9:15 pm

page 50
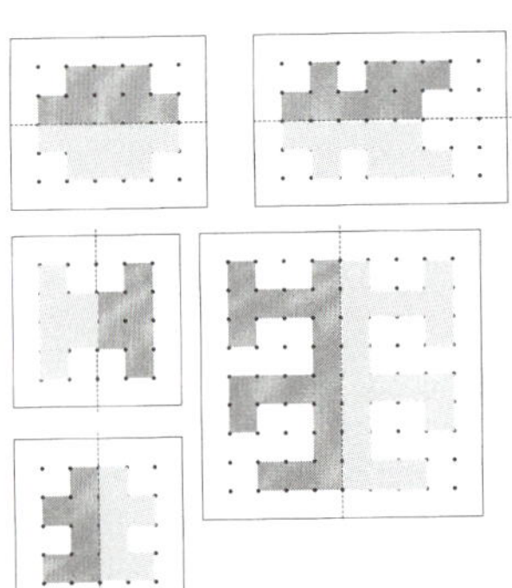

page 51
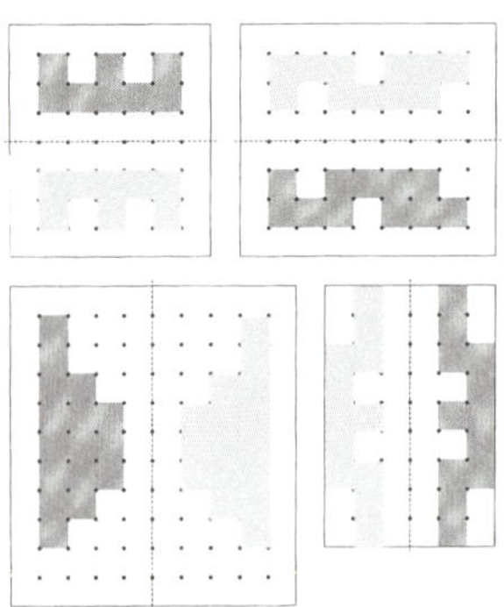

page 52
A $\frac{1}{2}$, half; **B** $\frac{1}{10}$, tenth; **C** $\frac{1}{5}$, fifth; **D** $\frac{1}{3}$, third; **E** $\frac{2}{3}$, two-thirds; **F** $\frac{1}{4}$, quarter

page 53
1 rectangle = $\frac{1}{10}$
10 rectangles = one whole
5 rectangles = $\frac{1}{2}$
2 rectangles = $\frac{1}{5}$
4 rectangles = $\frac{1}{3}$
8 rectangles = $\frac{2}{3}$
3 rectangles = $\frac{1}{4}$

page 54
A $\frac{7}{12}$; **B** $\frac{1}{4}$; **C** $\frac{5}{8}$; **D** $\frac{2}{5}$; **E** $\frac{1}{3}$; **F** $\frac{1}{6}$; **G** $\frac{3}{10}$; **H** $\frac{9}{20}$

page 55
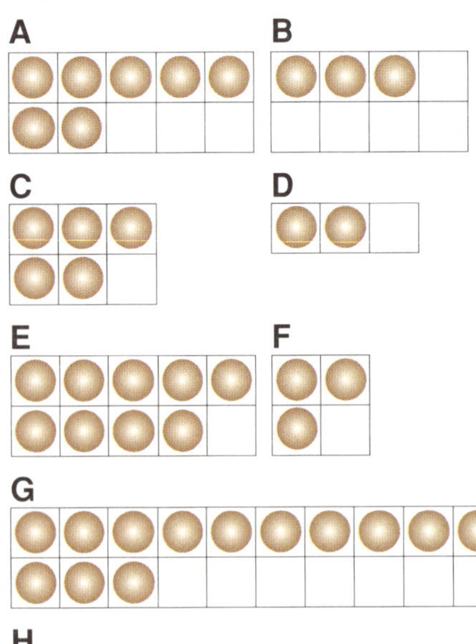

page 56
$\frac{1}{2}$ of 10 = 5; $\frac{1}{4}$ of 8 = 2; $\frac{1}{10}$ of 10 = 1; $\frac{1}{3}$ of 9 = 3
To find $\frac{1}{2}$, divide by 2; to find $\frac{1}{3}$, divide by 3; to find $\frac{1}{4}$, divide by 4; to find $\frac{1}{10}$ divide by 10

Answers

page 57
$\frac{1}{2}$: the circle has been cut into 2 pieces and we have 1
$\frac{1}{3}$: the circle has been cut into 3 pieces and we have 1
$\frac{1}{4}$: the circle has been cut into 4 pieces and we have 1
$\frac{2}{3}$: the circle has been cut into 3 pieces and we have 2
$\frac{3}{4}$: the circle has been cut into 4 pieces and we have 3

page 58

A
$\frac{1}{4} \to \frac{3}{4}$ $\frac{1}{6} \to \frac{5}{6}$ $\frac{1}{2} \to \frac{1}{2}$

$\frac{1}{3} \to \frac{2}{3}$ $\frac{1}{5} \to \frac{4}{5}$ $\frac{1}{8} \to \frac{7}{8}$

B
$\frac{3}{10} \to \frac{7}{10}$ $\frac{5}{8} \to \frac{3}{8}$ $\frac{2}{5} \to \frac{3}{5}$

$\frac{4}{7} \to \frac{3}{7}$ $\frac{2}{7} \to \frac{5}{7}$ $\frac{4}{9} \to \frac{5}{9}$

C
$\frac{3}{10} \to \frac{7}{10}$ $\frac{5}{10} \to \frac{5}{10}$ $\frac{9}{10} \to \frac{1}{10}$

$\frac{8}{10} \to \frac{2}{10}$ $\frac{6}{10} \to \frac{4}{10}$ $\frac{7}{10} \to \frac{3}{10}$

page 59

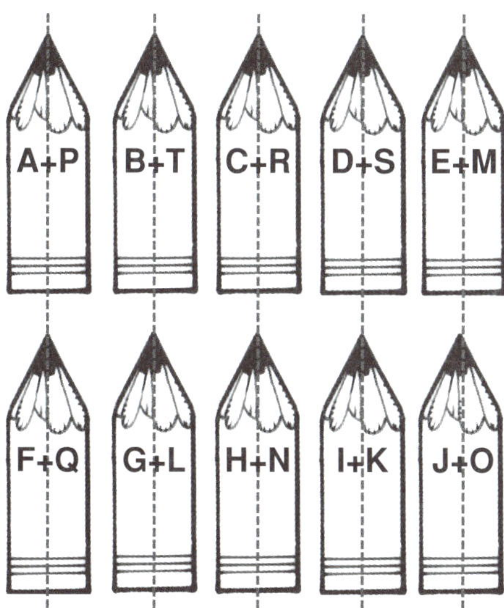

page 60
Cleaning the car: £3 each
Walking the dog: £1 each
Cleaning the kitchen: £4 each
Cleaning the windows: £9
9; 6; 3; 5

page 61
$\frac{1}{4}$, 3; $\frac{1}{10}$, 2, divide 20 by 10

page 62
A smallest, middle, largest
B middle, largest, smallest
C middle, smallest, largest

page 63
A ✗; B ✓; C ✓; D ✓; E ✓; F ✗; G ✓; H ✗; I ✗; J ✗; K ✗; L ✓;
M ✓; N ✓; O ✗; P ✓; Q ✓; R ✗; S ✗; T ✗; U ✓; V ✓; W ✓; X ✓

page 64
A $6, \frac{1}{6}$; **B** $8, \frac{1}{8}$; **C** $4, \frac{1}{4}$; **D** $3, \frac{1}{3}$

page 65
A Each person has 4 equal pieces
B Each person has 2 equal pieces
C Each person has 8 equal pieces
D Each person has 1 piece

page 66
A 2, 3; **B** 4, 6; **C** 10, 15

page 67
A   1 tube – 10 sweets
       2 tubes – 20 sweets
       3 tubes – 30 sweets
       4 tubes – 40 sweets
       5 tubes – 50 sweets
B   1 plate – 5 cookies
       2 plates – 10 cookies
       3 plates – 15 cookies
       4 plates – 20 cookies
       5 plates – 25 cookies
C   2 pieces – 1 extra
       4 pieces – 2 extra
       6 pieces – 3 extra
       8 pieces – 4 extra
       10 pieces – 5 extra
D   4 tokens – 1 monster
       8 tokens – 2 monsters
       12 tokens – 3 monsters
       16 tokens – 4 monsters
       20 tokens – 5 monsters

page 68
A $\frac{2}{3}$; **B** $\frac{1}{6}$; **C** $\frac{4}{9}$; **D** $\frac{6}{14}$ *or* $\frac{3}{7}$; **E** $\frac{3}{5}$; **F** $\frac{2}{6}$ *or* $\frac{1}{3}$; **G** $\frac{3}{4}$; **H** $\frac{2}{4}$ *or* $\frac{1}{2}$

page 69

A $\frac{6}{25}$; **B** $\frac{6}{36}$ *or* $\frac{1}{6}$; **C** $\frac{5}{25}$ *or* $\frac{1}{5}$, **D** $\frac{5}{50}$ *or* $\frac{1}{10}$

page 70
250ml, $\frac{1}{4}$
A $\frac{1}{2}$, 500ml; **B** $\frac{1}{4}$, 500ml; **C** $\frac{1}{2}$, 1500ml
10 cups hold 1 litre, so 30 cups hold 3 litres
1 litre fills 4 bowls, so 4 litres fill 16 bowls
about $\frac{1}{2}$ the children will get custard

page 71
A 1000m ÷ 2 = 500m
B 500m + 750m = 1250m
C 1250m + 750m = 2000m
25cm is $\frac{1}{4}$ of 1 metre
50cm is $\frac{1}{2}$ of 1 metre

page 72
A £5.20, £5.84, £6.25, £6.90, £7.65
B £1.25, £1.68, £2.14, £2.41, £2.56

page 73
A Mark (£4.20), James (£3.64),
   Mary (£3.25), Jenny (£2.98) ,
   Robin (£2.18), Rosie (£1.63)
B Carolyn (£4.52), Ben (£4.25),
   Alan (£3.49), Anne (£2.99),
   Colin (£2.36), Barbara (£2.15)

page 74
A $\frac{1}{4}$ 0.25
B $\frac{1}{2}$ 0.5
C $\frac{3}{4}$ 0.75
D $\frac{1}{2}$ 0.5
E 1 whole
F $\frac{1}{4}$ 0.25
G $\frac{3}{4}$ 0.75
H $\frac{1}{2}$ 0.5
I $\frac{1}{2}$ 0.5

page 75
$\frac{2}{10}$ 0.2; $\frac{3}{10}$ 0.3; $\frac{4}{10}$ 0.4; $\frac{9}{10}$ 0.9; $\frac{6}{10}$ 0.6; $\frac{8}{10}$ 0.8; $\frac{7}{10}$ 0.7; $\frac{1}{10}$ 0.1; $\frac{5}{10}$ or $\frac{1}{2}$ 0.5.

page 76
Answers from left to right: 7, 6, 15, 25, 4, 55, 10, 5, 3, 7, 6, 25, 8, 20, 80, 100, +, +, +, +, −, −, −, −

page 77
3 and 9, 3 and 5, 47, 24, 8, 8 and 16, 2 and 7, 14 and 7; 0, 5

page 78
The magic squares are 1 and 5

page 79

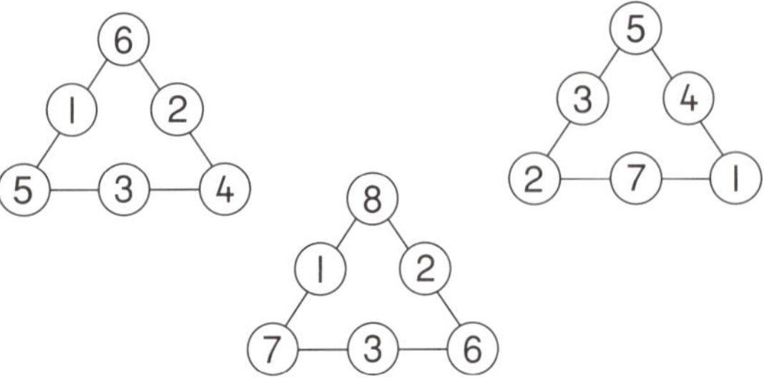

16	2	12	12	5	10
6	10	14	7	9	11
8	18	4	8	13	6

21	7	17	26	12	22
11	15	19	16	20	24
13	23	9	18	28	14

10	20	6	3	10	5
8	12	16	8	6	4
18	4	14	7	2	9

page 80
5 and 8, 7 and 5, 2 and 9, 6 and 8

page 81
6, 7 and 8; 15, 16 and 17; 7, 9 and 11; 16, 18, and 20

page 82
25 + 9 = 34, 35 − 14 = 21,
13 + 16 = 29, 36 − 12 = 24.
Various answers are possible, e.g., 33 + 3 = 36, 43 − 5 = 38,
35 + 17 = 52, 45 − 26 = 19

page 83
Various combinations are possible, e.g.,
2, 3, 5, 8 and 1, 4, 6, 7;
2, 3, 6, 7 and 1, 4, 5, 8
Various combinations are possible, e.g.,
9, 4, 2 and 8, 6, 1 and 3, 5, 7;
8, 3, 4 and 9, 5, 1 and 7, 6, 2

page 84   **page 85**

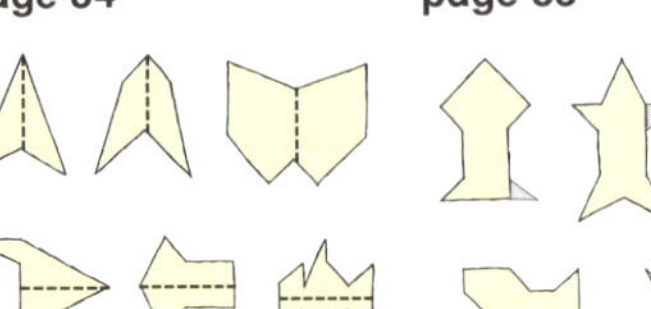
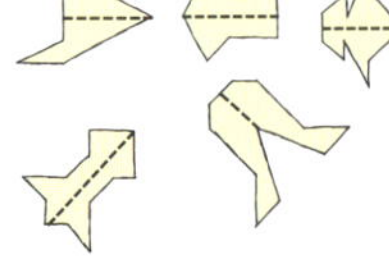
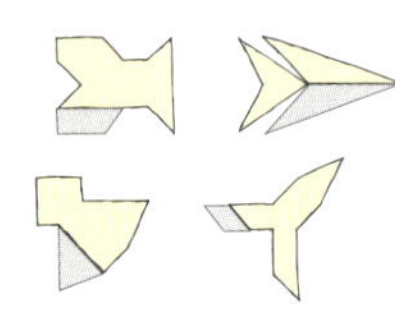

Answers

page 86
8 triangles, square-based pyramid, triangular prism

page 87
cube, cylinder, rectangular prism, hemisphere. A triangular prism has three faces that are rectangles and two identical triangular ends.

page 88
16 articles, 2 articles on each page, 240 sheets, 6 minutes

page 89
£30.00, 25 copies are unsold, £17.50, £9.50

page 90
Granny £5.00; Uncle £2.50; Friend £1.00; Dad 10p per length; total £13.50

page 91
5 x £2 = £10.00
20 x £1 = £20.00
10 x 50p = £5.00
10 x 20p = £2.00
20 x 10p = £2.00
20 x 5p = £1.00
50 x 2p = £1.00
100 x 1p = £1.00
Total £42.00
5 x £2 = 2 x £5 notes
20 x £1 = 2 x £10 notes
10 x 50p = 1 x £5 note
10 x 20p = 2 x £1 coins
20 x 10p = 2 x £1 coins
20 x 5p = 1 x £1 coin
50 x 2p = 1 x £1 coin
100 x 1p = 1 x £1 coin

page 92
£4.80, £17.75, £2.25, two 2 litre bottles are cheaper by 50p

page 93
£1.50 + £1.20 + £2.50 + 75p + 90p = £6.85. £3.15 change

page 94
20 x 5kg = 100kg, 6 or 7 apples in each bag, 20 bags, 40 bottles

page 95
potatoes 3kg, lemonade 1 litre or 2 litres, sugar 1kg; ribbon 25m, milk 1 litre or 2 litres, shoelaces 45cm

page 96
Tuesday, Thursday, 31, Thursday, 24 January, Friday, Friday

page 97
Gym Display, School Band, Gym Display, 20 minutes, 9.15 p m

page 98
6.00, 45 minutes, 50 minutes, 1 hour and 50 minutes, One Man and His Pig, Queen Street, Star Trip, 1 hour

page 99
8.15 am, 9.00 am, 45 minutes, 10 minutes, 9.10 am, 3 hours and 6 minutes, 2.15 pm, yes at 3.12 pm.

page 100
Joe brought 30 cakes, Tina brought 28 scones, Jack brought 25, 3 less than Tina. Yes, there were 20 + 40 + 45 = 105 chairs

page 101
Mary made £2.40, Jane made £3.00, Mike brought 63 sandwiches altogether. Carla bought apple tarts: £1.00 – 10p = 90p; 90 ÷ 6 = 15p

page 102
120 boys, 30 boys like football, 40 girls like football, one-quarter

page 103
One-quarter use blue ropes, half prefer the climbing frame, one-third prefer the scramble net. 12 prefer a longer playtime, two-fifths eat fruit.

page 104

+	1	2	3	4	5	6	7	8	9	10
1	2	3	4	5	6	7	8	9	10	11
2	3	4	5	6	7	8	9	10	11	12
3	4	5	6	7	8	9	10	11	12	13
4	5	6	7	8	9	10	11	12	13	14
5	6	7	8	9	10	11	12	13	14	15
6	7	8	9	10	11	12	13	14	15	16
7	8	9	10	11	12	13	14	15	16	17
8	9	10	11	12	13	14	15	16	17	18
9	10	11	12	13	14	15	16	17	18	19
10	11	12	13	14	15	16	17	18	19	20

Answer	Frequency
1–4	6
5–8	22
9–12	36
13–16	26
17–20	10

9–12 because all the numbers are part of a number bond that makes 9–12; 1–4 because they are small numbers, there are not many number bonds that make 1–4; 1 does not appear in the answers because the lowest addition is 1 + 1 = 2

page 105

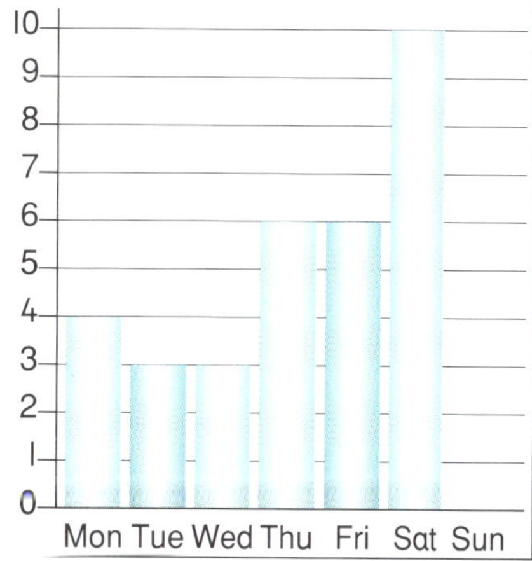

Saturday; 10; Sunday because no TVs were sold; 18

page 106
12, 6, 25, 17; lorry = 1, car = 3, motorbike = 2; total = 6

page 107
fish = HH II; starfish = HH I; octopus = II; sea snail = HH HH III
house = HH III; chimney-pot = HH HH II; window = HH HH HH I;
door = HH III

page 108

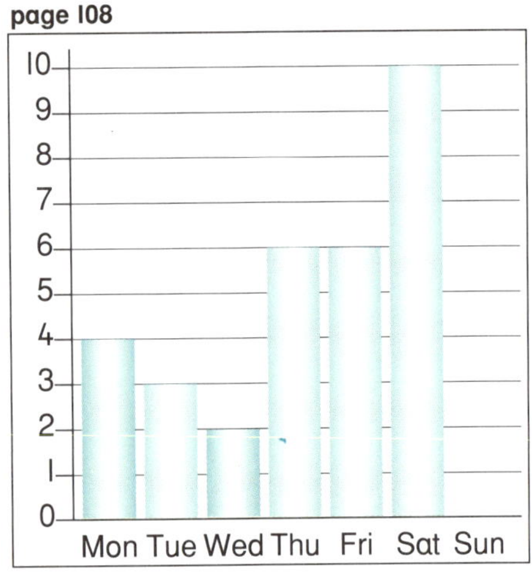

The first Thursday and the second Sunday because they watched lots of TV. The family went out on the first Sunday because no TV was watched. The family watched most TV in week I

page 109

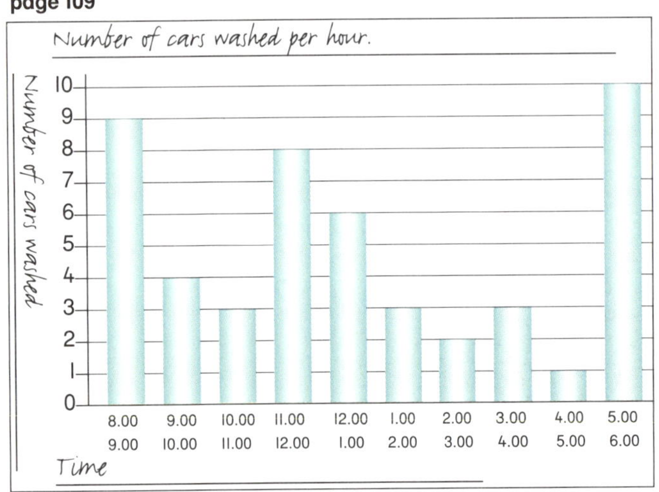

page 110

Morning and evening; it is when people are travelling to and from school and work

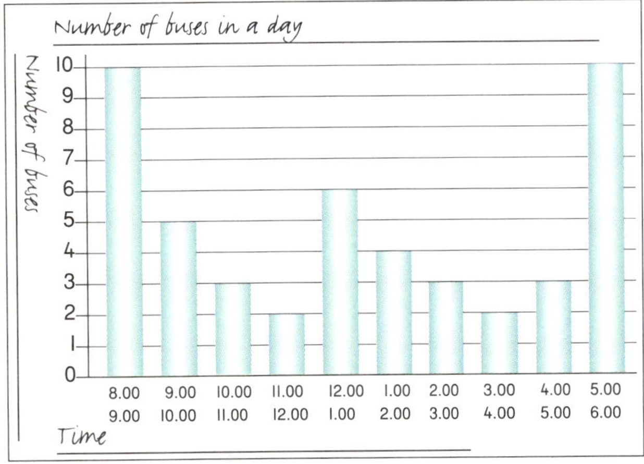

page III

9; Mon = 9, Tues = 12; Wed = 7; Thu = 6; Fri = 5; Sat = 8; Sun = 10
Tuesday; Thursday; Friday

page II2

30; 5; 15. Jan = 30; Feb = 20; Mar = 65; Apr = 10; May = 20; Jun = 5; Jul = 35; Aug = 55; Sep = 45; Oct = 15; Nov = 5; Dec = 25

page II3

January = $2\frac{1}{4}$ pictograms; February = $1\frac{3}{4}$; March = $1\frac{1}{2}$; April = $1\frac{1}{4}$; May = 1; June = 1; July = $\frac{1}{2}$; August = 0; September = 2; October = $2\frac{1}{2}$; November = $2\frac{3}{4}$; December = $3\frac{1}{4}$.
The weather is colder; August because no hot dinners were sold; pictograms can be clearer because there is less counting but you may have other reasons

page II4

60 crossings = 3 pictograms; 100 = 5; 120 = 6; 140 = 7; 160 = 8; 180 = 9; 15 = $\frac{3}{4}$; 25 = $1\frac{1}{4}$; 40 = 2; 110 = $5\frac{1}{2}$

page II5

Jan = 20, Feb = 45, March = 65, April = 50, May = 70, June = 80, July = 95, Aug = 100, Sept = 80, Oct = 75, Nov = 60, Dec = 15.
December; August; April; June and September

page II6

Intervals of 5 or 10

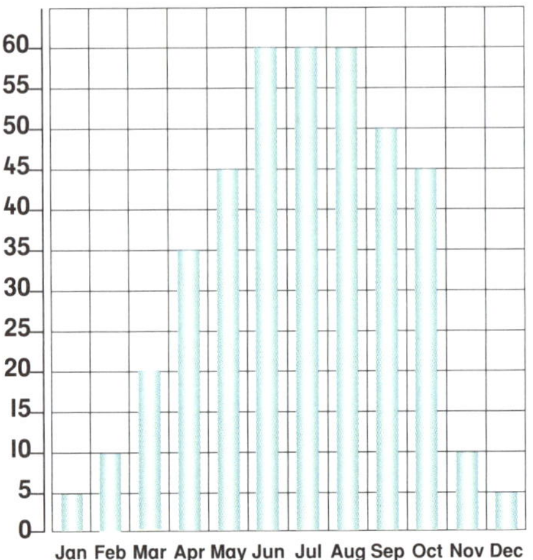

page II7

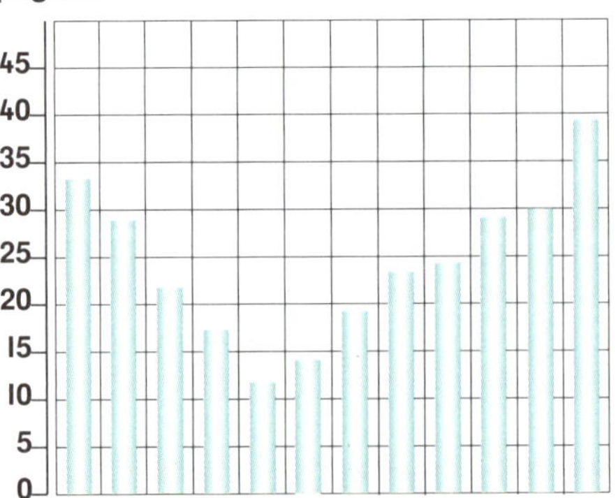

Christmas and the New Year sales.

page II8

soaps; 4: cartoons, dramas, soaps, films; horror; films; dramas; soaps because they have the most viewers

page II9

nut roast; nut roast 11:55; potatoes 12:20; gravy 12:55; carrots 12:50; sprouts 12:40; peas 12:45; roast potatoes 12:10

page I2I

Computer games and swimming are most popular; watching TV least